Talking With Flutists

DONALD PECK
MARY LOUISE POOR
JAMES PAPPOUTSAKIS
THOMAS NYFENGER
HENRY ZLOTNIK
EUGENIA ZUKERMAN
BERNARD GOLDBERG
MURRAY PANITZ

BY PILAR ESTEVAN   volume 2

©1978
ENVOLVE MUSIC COMPANY
Publishers
International Copyright Secured
Any copying or adaption of these works
without the consent of the copyright owners
is an infringement of copyright.
Made in USA

Library of Congress Number 76-13793
ISBN 0-89495-001-X

ABOUT TALKING WITH FLUTISTS

You are now holding what I consider one of the most important books about music and musicians in the last 50 years. —A book which will be read by thousands of people of all ages.

Why? Simply, because men, woman and children, the world over have something in common - music - and an interest in the people who make music.

They not only make beautiful music, but shape the lives of many of us with their spoken philosophy. Each master magnificently communicates his thoughts through the expert questions of Ms. Estevan.

This book is so packed with the marvels of each and every artist that all the adjectives cannot correctly express my personal feelings.

I have learned much from these artists.

I am sure you will, too.

Eugene Frank
Publisher

BIOGRAPHY

Pilar Estevan, born in New York and reared in Connecticut received her education in Spain at the University of Valencia and studied voice and theatre at the Conservatory of Theatre and Music in Barcelona.

She studied writing with Robert Penn Warren at Yale University, acting with Stella Adler and voice with Sue Seton in New York.

"Talking With Flutists" is Ms. Estevan's first venture into publishing. Her other credits include "the most promising actress" at the Mediterranean Theatre Festival in Spain, her role as Polly in "The Three Penny Opera and numerous acting and singing appearances.

This edition of "Talking With Flutists" is the first of a three edition series by Ms. Estevan.

She presently resides in Connecticut with her husband, flutist, Robert Dick.

Photograph by Eugene Cook

CONTENTS

DONALD PECK

DONALD PECK

Donald Peck, the principal flutist of the Chicago Symphony Orchestra, came to Chicago in 1957 at the invitation of Fritz Reiner and has continued on with Jean Martinon and Sir Georg Solti. He has performed with many great conductors, including Stokowski, Stravinsky, Ormandy, Beecham, Boulez, Walter, Hindemith, Szell, Ozawa and Leinsdorf. Mr. Peck is often a soloist with the CSO in Chicago and on tour. To date he has performed at over 50 concerts in this capacity. He is featured on recordings of the Chicago Symphony on RCA, Angel and London. In the Autumn of 1974, Mr. Peck toured the musical capitols of Europe for 6 weeks with the Chicago Symphony including Paris, London, Berlin, Vienna, Helsinki, Milan, Stockholm and Edinburgh on the itinerary. Mr. Peck is also musically active outside of Chicago. He is often guest flutist with other symphony orchestras in the United States. In 1963 he performed at the Casals Festival in Puerto Rico, with concerts in San Juan, Santo Domingo in the Dominican Republic, and at Carnegie Hall in New York. In July of 1970 and 1971 he was featured soloist at the Carmel Festival in California playing solo works from the Baroque and Classical repertoire. In the summer of 1972, he went to Australia where he worked under the auspicies of the Australian Broadcasting Commission. He recorded the Mozart Flute Concerti for broadcast over Radio Australia and worked with the National Training Orchestra in Sydney where he gave lectures, Master Classes, flute clinics and coaching in Woodwind Ensemble. Mr. Peck is also active in the field of Chamber Music and solo flute recitals in many cities of the United States including New York, Philadelphia, Washington, Seattle, Kansas City, Baltimore and Chicago. In 1965 he gave his debut flute recital at Town Hall in New York City and has since returned there twice with his own group, *Trio Concertante*. In Chicago, in addition to his solo flute recitals, Mr. Peck performs often as a member of the Chicago Symphony Chamber Music Ensemble.

Donald Peck is on the faculty of DePaul University in Chicago where he teaches flute and woodwind ensemble. He also gives Master Classes and flute clinics as guest lecturer at other colleges and universities.

He received his early musical training in Seattle, in his native State of Washington. As a youth he played in the Seattle Youth Symphony Orchestra and the semi-professional Seattle Philharmonic. While in his early teens he was accepted as a member of the Seattle Symphony Orchestra then under the directorship of Manuel Rosenthal. When he was 18 he received a scholarship to the Curtis Institute of Music in Philadelphia where he studied flute with William Kincaid, and ensemble with Marcel Tabuteau. Between graduation and his Chicago tenure he played with the Washington National Symphony Orchestra, the Kansas City Philharmonic, the Santa Fe Opera Orchestra, and the U.S. Marine Band and Symphony Orchestra in Washington, D.C.

He has served on the Board of Directors of the National Flute Association for two years and for the 1977 convention in San Francisco he served as Chairman of the Program Committee.

In the Spring of 1977, he toured Japan for a month with the Chicago Symphony Orchestra. Donald Peck has also recorded the Bach Brandenburg Concerti Nos. 2 and 5 with James Levine, harpsichord and conductor, Samuel Magad, violin, and members of the Chicago Symphony Orchestra from the Ravinia Festival for RCA Records.

SETTING

"Can we do the interview in Central Park? It's my day off and the sun is great."

"No batteries for my cassette."

"Okay, come up. The room is neat."

Standing in the doorway of his Park Sheraton Hotel room in New York, Mr. Peck, slight and intense, looked straight at me; his blue eyes alert, at a glance, sized me up. "Hello," he said in a light clear voice and showed me into the room. I sat down in an armchair by a lamp and placed the cassette on the bureau next to a folded copy of the *Daily News*. On the bed was a brown leather suitcase opened and neatly packed. The television was off. The orange and black drapes were drawn wide and the window which faced rows and rows of other windows was opened letting in a spring breeze but no sun.

Light, like a darting animal, Mr. Peck reached out for a chair and sat down facing me, crossed his legs and cupped his chin, his palm turned outward and his slender fingers slightly curled. He wore a beige linen jacket with red plaid silk lining, a white nylon shirt, a green and blue paisley tie, black trousers and shoes with silver buckles. "The jacket is from Saks," he said.

Handsome, with a high forehead and cheekbones, thin lips which at the start held a pursed, expectant smile and dark hair which is thinning and threaded with grey, it is his eyes that dominate and could rivet you.

When he relaxed, mid-way through the hour and a half interview, a gentleness surfaced and his voice became softer, as when speaking of "the beauty of the orchestra," and then with a steely directness he spoke about discipline and "picking yourself up by the back of the neck and doing it." He listened intently to the questions and answered with clarity and ease. As he hardly gestured, one felt a self-screening, a struggle to bridle the sheerness of his sensitivity yet one also felt he would be excellent at a game of darts.

INTERVIEW

P.E. From the beginning, your musical career took off like a roller coaster. You played in the Seattle Youth Symphony Orchestra, the Seattle Philharmonic, the Seattle Syphony Orchestra, and when you were 18 you received a scholarship to the Curtis Institute of Music in Philadelphia. And then on to play with the Washington National Symphony Orchestra, the Kansas City Philharmonic, the Sante Fe Opera Orchestra and even the U.S. Marine Band. How did you arrive in the first chair of the Chicago Symphony?

PECK I let the roller coaster carry me, actually taking the line of least resistance. I worked hard to be ready if an opportunity came by, and when it did, I took it. If you fight something or push too hard for something, I don't think it's quite right. It seems that if you just take it the way it comes, you will get there. Do you know what I'm saying?

P.E. If you have to try too hard you will miss; if you aim with too much tension, you will miss your target.

PECK It's the same idea. In fact, it sometimes goes against what we think we want because we have an idea of what we want, and the obvious path doesn't always go that way and we are upset by that at the time.

P.E. Have you ever encountered such a situation?

PECK I did in 1962. My teacher was William Kincaid. When he retired, I was offered the first flute position in Philadelphia. I had only been in Chicago for four years then. I wanted to go to Philadelphia right or wrong. So I signed a two year contract with Philadelphia but my orchestra would not release me from my contract in Chicago. Things have changed now. The contracts are more fluid. I can't imagine any orchestra forcing you to stay anymore. But Chicago really forced me to stay then. I am not unhappy now, but I was very unhappy then. I might have really made a mess of things by fighting and striving and pushing more than I did. It was quite exciting, though, at the time. Headline in the paper: "ONE FLUTIST, TWO ORCHESTRAS"!

P.E. Was the contract legally binding?

PECK No, probably not. I had gone to a lawyer and there were things about the contract that were dubious. But these contracts had never been taken to a court before.

P.E. It would have been a first in Orchestral history?

PECK I think so. A union contract taken to a court; it would have created a big scene. There was nothing finally that I could do, and of course it didn't matter all that much, so I decided to stay in Chicago.

P.E. You believe in fate more so than self determination?

PECK I think it's important to realize yourself and your potential honestly and not push beyond what you are capable of doing. If you do, you will be very unhappy your whole life. Certainly someone may want to sing *Tristan und Isolde* at the Metropolitan Opera, but if you have a small voice it can't be done. You have to realize what you can and cannot do. It's not only important to realize yourself and know what you can and can't do, but also to *accept* this. Accept the area where you have the potential or the lack of potential, then you will be happier. If you don't accept who you are, you are constantly fighting yourself, you are constantly churning inside; you will be a very unhappy man or woman. To realize who you are, you must adapt, and then you can live. I think the reason for many problems is that people are not realistic about themselves.

P.E. Did anyone in your family play the flute?

PECK No, but my sister played the piano. She had a trio with a flute and a violin, and the flutist was a girl who now plays in the Boston Symphony, Lois Schaefer. She is a marvelous flute player; she started me on the flute. I was about 11 at the time. I was interested in the clarinet, but my sister pushed me into playing the flute because of her friendship with Lois. I am glad that I went along with that push.

P.E. Did you feel any special kinship with the flute?

PECK No. I don't think there was any great explosion. But I do think there must be something to talent in a certain area. It's not just something that is acquired. Like most musicians, I had a love for music, even when I was very young. I would sit at the piano as a little boy and play, although, of course, I didn't play anything anybody wanted to hear. I was from a small town in Washington state. My folks were completely unmusical. We didn't have any records. I just always loved music; it was all very natural. I really think it's not difficult to find one's proper niche today.

P.E. But there are more distractions, more choices to be made.

PECK Nowadays a child can hear everything; there are so many books and things that are geared to the child, like contests and grants and so on.

P.E. What were your lessons with William Kincaid and Marcel Tabuteau like?

PECK Marcel Tabuteau was the chamber music coach at Curtis. He had a wonderful ensemble class where all the woodwind players got together. He was incredibly intimidating and he meant to be. He wanted to separate the men from the boys. If you couldn't shape up, ship out.

P.E. Shape up how?

PECK Do things exactly right, technically and musically. You know, there is an incredible amount of anarchistic, sloppy playing. They come in, "boom," and they get out, "boom." No finesse. They only practice the fingers. Tabuteau was trying to develop an ensemble sense. Some people couldn't take it and they would drop out, and that's fine. They should leave if they are not of that calibre. There are lots of people around who still can't make it because there are a lot of things that go into it besides talent such as hard work, discipline and control. You have to have steady nerves. Even if you are nervous, you must never sound that way and you have to be able to play exactly what's there.

P.E. What kind of music did you listen to in your youth?

PECK In those days, I listened to the radio, to the New York Philharmonic and the NBC Symphony Orchestra under Arturo Toscanini. I think at that time I was listening differently than I would now.

P.E. How do you listen differently to music today?

PECK Then, I just heard the overall sound, uncritical and unknowing. Today when I go to a concert, the first part of it is very calculating and critical in a technical sense. Two orchestras I heard recently are the Berlin and the Vienna Orchestras. The Berlin Philharmonic came with Von Karajan. At first it was a new tone; it's different from any in America, so you first have to adapt to it and listen to all the instruments, the flute, the oboe, and how they blend, and then you get to the brass, and then you listen to the strings.

P.E. But what about your musical experience?

PECK That's it. It takes me a long time to get to that. By the end of the first movement of a symphony I have finally gotten used to the new sound and style and I start to enjoy the music. I suddenly have gotten completely enthralled. The Berlin Philharmonic gave a glorious concert. I absolutely loved it. Now, the Vienna Philharmonic came, and again I first listened to the Orchestra very critically, but I did not enjoy it. I found the Orchestra rough and coarse, and this hampered my enjoyment of the music because it didn't come out sounding beautiful except, perhaps, for their lovely string sound.

P.E. Do you feel music should always be beautiful?

PECK I like things to be beautiful. Of course, there is some music where an ugly tone is required for some special effect or reason, but I feel that overall it should be an uplifting experience, not grey, rough or mundane.

P.E. What were your lessons with Kincaid like?

PECK Kincaid was a great scientist. He could fathom your problems and suggest cures. He taught each student in a different way. After all, each person needs different help for his special problem. He was always a gentleman and a great inspiration, not by being dramatic in a personal way, but just by his playing and his knowledge. It was a great experience for me.

P.E. Would you say that William Kincaid established the American flute tradition?

PECK Yes. Kincaid made the style of flute playing in America, which started with George Barrere from France. Barrere taught Kincaid.

P.E. What was Kincaid's approach to the flute?

PECK He didn't want to be "flutey" or "birdie". He wanted some importance and depth to the sound. His tone became darker, deeper and fuller. It was a tone that wasn't forced out of the flute. Some of the Europeans seem to force the tone out of the flute. It's super intense all the time. Kincaid got away from that.

P.E. How did Kincaid achieve this ease in his playing?

PECK He didn't pull back on his lips so tightly. The resistance came from a small pursing of the lips at the center and the tone sounded very natural. He changed a bit over the years. Everybody changes. When they first started to use vibrato, they all had very fast vibratos because they didn't know how to do it otherwise. Finally Kincaid developed a slower vibrato, more like a singer. The fast vibrato was like uh-uh-uh-uh-uh; sort of staccato instead of a wave. Kincaid made many changes: changes in flutes, which altered the sound. He had an incredibly sharp mind. Fortunately he was musically oriented so he didn't sound studied or academic. He was the ultimate of the tasteful player—never a gauche thing, never slopping all over the stage for the sake of an effect, and never moving his body around too much. He didn't want to detract from the music. When you sat there and heard him play, it was exquisite. The only word for him was exquisite.

P.E. You mentioned that you played the piano. How did playing the piano help your musical understanding and your learning of the flute?

PECK Playing the piano helped my sight-reading and my understanding of harmonies and chords. I'm sure you, as a singer, are helped by the piano. It helped me generally to learn music.

P.E. How did you achieve a fully projected tone that reaches out into the hall, hits dead center and is not spready?

PECK I learned it first by listening to Kincaid up close and then hearing him in the hall. Then I would know that such and such a tone up close achieves such and such an effect out front. After that it was a matter of trial and error on my own. The tone should be out of the mass of sound of the orchestra. Singers experience this, too. If you look at them on the stage you would swear that the tone is not coming from them, but it's ringing all around in the hall. Other players or singers, you see them on the stage and the tone is coming *from* them. You hear the tone *from* the stage with the other instruments. That's one thing the flute can do in a really big orchestra, project. Some instruments can't. They can play loudly, but it's always coming from the stage. One learns that too open a sound doesn't project because there is no center or core. On the other hand, if you squeeze the tone, you confine it and cut out many of the overtones that make the sound project.

P.E. Did you create a catalog of tones?

PECK Yes, in my mind. I've been experimenting with tone and different colors of tone.

P.E. Could you tell me in what ways you have experimented with tone, with colors of tone and how you apply them to your playing?

PECK I don't feel that one sound fits all music. I didn't consciously go out to find different qualities. I just suddenly realized that I was using different tones for different music. Then I observed what I was doing and catalogued them in my mind. For example, I would use a thinner, brighter tone for Mozart and then a darker, deeper sound for Debussy or a full, round and fairly bright tone for Brahms and so on. The sound changes are made by varying the throat cavity, forming different syllables; or the raising or lowering on the lip of the embouchure plate, or turning the opening in and out. Vibrato is also involved but most of all it is in the mind. The body will adjust for you if you have a concept in the mind. I feel there is a puff of air right out in front of my lips or a curl or a pearl right out in front of my lips. You just feel the tone zinging out.

P.E. Do you think it is important to play long tones?

PECK I don't think holding one long tone does much for musicianship but I do play long tones sometimes myself because I notice it does cure problems on a particular tone. For example, if we are to play *Afternoon of a Faun* by Debussy, I practice a lot of C sharps, because *Afternoon of a Faun* includes many, many C sharps and it's one of the worst notes on the instrument.

P.E. Does this follow your idea of having a mental concept?

PECK Yes. You have to know what you want first or at least have some concept. Just tell yourself, "I want to have the most scrumptious sound, just dripping with quality." In the beginning, you'll start to play your long tones, but it won't sound so scrumptious, but then you'll play the C sharp again and again, and maybe you'll lip it up or lip it down, or adjust in some other way, and before long, in a day, or two days, or a week, you'll be getting a great C sharp.

P.E. Keep at it.

PECK Yes. You know, people don't believe that. I tell them, let your brain do it for you. It will work out the problem.

P.E. Trust your talent. Once you get yourself out of the way, your talent flows.

PECK Right. Work hard, but with direction and purpose.

P.E. Since you are so busy, how can you manage to arrange time for your practicing, and what do you practice?

PECK It depends on what we are going to play. I don't practice everything. Only those pieces that might need it. I did both of the Mozart flute concertos with the Chicago Symphony — Number 1 with Raphael Kubelik conducting, and Number 2 with James Levine conducting. I had to brush up on them so I practiced a bit more than I might ordinarily have. I don't believe in wasting time by just going through a piece of music, going through everything. I look at the music and find the part that is hard and I merely practice that — the hard part.

P.E. You joined your first professional orchestra, the Seattle Symphony, when you were a teenager. How did you manage to jump in and learn the orchestral repertoire?

PECK It was hectic. I hadn't really played that much, so for a few years it was very strenuous until I basically covered the general repertoire. After that, all I had to do was learn a new piece that came out, and the whole orchestra was learning it too, so it didn't matter. But in the beginning it was very difficult to jump in and play all the standard repertoire.

P.E. What skills supported you through this hectic period?

PECK A good basic schooling and technique. I practised a lot and I had nerves of steel.

P.E. How did you organize your practicing to go about learning all those pieces?

PECK Again, I just practiced the hard parts, using my time there. For the rest of the music, I relied on my general technique. That would be my work of the day, combined with a lot of scale work and excercises, which I still use, especially on a warm-up basis to maintain my general technique.

P.E. Your prime objective, then, was to build up your technique so that you could play almost anything without having to practice.

PECK Absolutely. Too many of the students just want to learn solos, and too many teachers just want to teach them the solos. I think that's a mistake because they should do the excercises and *learn the flute* so that you can play the pieces without having to practice them so much. You have to know your instrument. In the orchestra we play too much music to go home every night and practice every piece. I remember once when I had first joined the Chicago Symphony, we were doing Tchaikovsky's 4th Symphony. Fritz Reiner was conducting, and he asked, "Does anybody want to rehearse?" and everyone yelled, "NO!" So I played the concert without a rehearsal, and that was very hard with Reiner; you just didn't go out and make a mistake with him on the podium.

P.E. You tried out your nerves of steel?

PECK Yes, that's the discipline I was talking about earlier.

P.E. How do you define discipline?

PECK If you are in a pinch, you still must come through and not fall apart. It requires you to grab ahold of the back of your own neck and just do it. The technique of getting through is a cold and calculating thing, assuming of course that you have previously learned your instrument.

P.E. For what purpose do you ask your students to use a metronome?

PECK Not so much to see how fast they can play, but how steady. You will find that most students want to slow down in the slow part and in the fast parts they want to rush. It is especially annoying when they slow down under the guise of being expressive, artistic. To be really artistic is to play within the confines of what the composer wrote. As for rhythm, you can play rubato and still be in rhythm.

P.E. How do you play rubato and still remain in rhythm?

PECK The pulse of the beat goes on constantly under you, and on top of that you may play around a bit with the meter; but you always come out on the next bar on time. You are not slowing down the whole tempo. You will be a bit faster here and you make it up by being a bit slower there, but you come out on time. To slow down the whole piece arbitrarily because you want to be artistic is being corny and unartistic. It requires absolutely nothing to be able to do that. Anybody can do that. But to do it in rhythm — that's where the art is.

P.E. In what ways have you changed your ideas about phrasing over the years?

PECK I notice that when I was younger I would take more liberty with types of phrasing, doing things that I wouldn't think of doing now.

P.E. You were more daring? Have you become more conventional?

PECK No. It's just that I consider too many liberties to be gauche now. You mature musically and this affects your technique because your ideas of what you want to come out of the instrument change. It changes because of experiences and challenges that you have accepted and come out of well.

P.E. What do you think of rotating players in the orchestra and of more interchange among flutists of different orchestras?

PECK This idea of rotating orchestral players sounds wonderful, but it doesn't always work well. If a marvelous string quartet rehearses and plays for years, they play like one man. Ideally, that is what should be happening in the orchestra. So if you change one person in the woodwind section, everything is thrown off. We do have a rotation system in our orchestra however. The first chair man decides who plays what during the week. For example, if I want to take off a piece that doesn't require my special services, I can give it to another player. It's almost necessary now with our very busy schedules and long seasons but it is not always the best artistic idea.

P.E. Where is the control in the orchestra?

PECK There is a variety of control. The musical director has a certain amount, the manager has a certain amount, and the orchestra committee has a certain amount, and of course, the first chair person has a certain type of control in his section. It is all spread around. I will be curious to see what happens in the future with the orchestras. The same thing is happening in the opera houses. The stage directors are taking over more and more power, and the set designer and so on.

P.E. It is a director's era in opera?

PECK You cannot get a top-notch conductor to conduct an opera. Carlo Maria Giulini will not go near an opera house anymore. Sir Georg Solti does only one opera in Paris every year, and maybe one in London and he hasn't been in New York or Chicago or San Francisco for years. When Von Karajan conducts an opera, it is only if he has absolute and final control of the whole project.

P.E. What we are speaking about is power.

PECK Yes, it is.

P.E. Does having power interest you?

PECK No. I have never thought about it or worried about it. It doesn't interest me.

P.E. What do you enjoy about playing in the orchestra?

PECK The first thing is the variety of the repertoire of different periods and its beauty. It is incredible. Secondly, it is always a challenge to fit your part in and to help somebody else sound beautiful when he has a solo and to come out beautifully when you have it. To put it all together is quite a challenge, and an honor.

P.E. You have played under Leopold Stokowski, Igor Stravinsky, Eugene Ormandy, Bruno Walter, Sir Georg Solti and many more. What have you learned from these conductors?

PECK It is hard to say what each one drew out of me, but each one drew out a different tone quality, which I find uncanny and incredibly interesting. Sir Georg Solti, for example, has a more brilliant, thinner tone. I always think of it as brilliant sky-blue. It can be very sweet at times, but it is not a fat sound. I find myself playing that way without thinking about it. It is the arm motions he gives, perhaps, or the tightness across his shoulders. Now, when Carlo Maria Giulini comes, he achieves a great, broad, deep tone. I think of that as a lustrous maroon. I find myself playing fuller and darker with him. Eugene Ormandy draws his tones, Stokowski, Leinsdorf, they're all different.

P.E. What do you mean by "drawing his tone"?

PECK The conductors don't usually talk about tone. It is just the muscle reaction and mental reaction, too, of the orchestra men to the conductor — his personality, his gestures, his phrasing. The conductor evokes his sound without really trying. It's a mystery.

P.E. What was your musical experience with Igor Stravinsky like?

PECK Stravinsky was quite old when he came to Chicago. He was eighty and somewhat feeble at the time. We did do some recording with him. Robert Craft rehearsed, generally, and Stravinsky would then take part in the final rehearsal and in the concert. We would basically do what Craft wanted us to do in the concert.

P.E. When Stravinsky conducted, what do you feel he drew from the orchestra?

PECK Igor Stravinsky wanted his music played with fierce attention to the rhythm, and with a *secco*, dry quality. He was not a romanticist.

P.E. You have traveled extensively in Europe with

the Chicago Symphony. What have you observed about European orchestras regarding their attitude and proficiency?

PECK I believe that the musicians the world over have the same goals: to play great performances, both musically and technically.

P.E. How do European conductors regard our Orchestras?

PECK They love our orchestras. Our orchestras are the best in the world. We have to be chauvinistic about that because it is realistic. Europe does not have a major orchestra in the American sense. We have our Big Five, and Berlin is the only orchestra in Europe that is in this class. Europe does have some very fine orchestras, like Amsterdam or London, but these are merely the equivalent of some of our finer, secondary orchestras.

P.E. What makes our orchestras great?

PECK It is what Marcel Tabuteau was trying to teach us: discipline and adaptability. A conductor can come here and ask us to play a certain way and we will do it immediately. European conductors are impressed with our flexibility and the ease with which we adapt to each different style. The Viennese can play their music better than anyone but they can't play some other music as well. The French orchestras play French music gorgeously, of course, but do you really want to hear them play Mahler? Although our orchestras are old, we don't have this built-in tradition, so we have had to learn a variety of styles and therefore, we are more flexible.

P.E. How do you handle a conductor who is difficult?

PECK We basically have a nice orchestra. There have been very few mutinous moments, but sometimes it does reach the point where you can't play well because of a bad conductor, even though you are trying to play your best. It might come out sounding forced or just plain bad. You are unhappy because you don't want to sound bad. You want to sound beautiful. So when the conductor makes us sound less than our ideal high standard, we really resent it and he does not get his best concert. It is through no fault of ours, because we do try. But we can't overcome him: his bad beat, or his over-conducting, or his gauche musicianship.

P.E. How do you work for resonance and a singing tone?

PECK By *thinking* of the quality I want and by letting the flute speak naturally. I begin with a natural low-register tone. I don't pump it or force it. The high notes are really overtones of the low notes. If you then lip-up a beautiful low note by changing the direction of the air stream, you have no choice but to get a good high note. I think this, then, makes for a natural resonance.

P.E. What are the differences in tone you have found amongst platinum, gold, and silver flutes?

PECK I liked the platinum flute at one time because our Orchestra Hall in Chicago used to be very alive and very bright. Platinum is a dense metal so the tone is dark, and in this bright hall the platinum flute sounded gorgeous. It had a rich dark tone. I prefer a darker qual-ity tone because I don't want to sound "flutey" or "birdie," either. Also, the response on platinum is very quick because the metal is drawn so thin. It requires less air to blow, although it will take more air if you want to give it. But when our hall was remodeled a few years ago, it became very dull and dead, so I had to switch to something brighter and silver is brighter. I use that now. It also can sound warm without being muddy. For my taste, gold is muddy; too mellow. I also find it rather hard to change the tone color on gold. It is just too pretty all the time. But don't forget that each player will tend to change the results of each metal by the way in which he plays.

P.E. Does music begin on the first or second note for you?

PECK I feel it begins on the second note because it seems to be a natural grouping. One/—two, three, four . . . One/—two, three, four . . . One. I don't like to be blocked: one/two/three/four, /one/two/three/four /one/two/three/four/.

P.E. Then, taking a breath after the first beat of the next measure would give the illusion of ongoing time. And if you took a breath, no one would notice it.

PECK Hopefully. There are always exceptions to rules, of course.

P.E. Do you approach the high notes at the beginning of the phrase or at the end of a crescendo?

PECK I can answer that very well. In Brahm's *Fourth Symphony,* for example, there is a high F sharp in the big flute solo in the last movement. I feel that the higher note in any interval is determined by the previous note. The note before the high F sharp in Brahms is D sharp. If I have a good D sharp intensity before that F sharp, I merely carry the D sharp intensity through to the F sharp. I won't begin any new intensity suddenly on the F sharp.

P.E. What do you mean by "new intensity"?

PECK I mean, I won't push the breath. I merely lip-up into the F sharp from the D sharp with exactly the same air and tone with which I left the D sharp. I don't have a sudden spurt of air on the high F sharp. But, then, if I wish to expand on the high note, the F sharp, I can, but it must come after I arrive at the note. I don't believe in plowing into notes. The high note should be approached through the intensity of the previous note. It must be built.

P.E. How do you work for smoothness in your playing?

PECK I practice and I don't push the keys down abruptly. One should *depress* them. It's a slow action. With my students I have a motto, and it's called "one air." To me the air is somewhat like the bow of the violin, and it goes and it goes and each note doesn't have its own little air. Just like the violin. Each note doesn't have its own little bow. You merely move the fingers and perhaps change the direction of the air. But the air itself, the intensity of it, remains the same. If you wish to become louder it would be a gradual increase in intensity. But there will be no abrupt puffing or backing away.

Many people like to back away and then ooze out on the high notes, or something corny like that, or thay like to force out the high note with an expulsion of air.

P.E. You said that each note doesn't have its own little air.

PECK Yes. The air goes. It moves continuously. You play *on top* of the air — a constant air, not a pulsing air. Many times I would like to have a very smooth phrase, so I will hold one note and sing the phrase in my mind while I'm holding that one note.

P.E. How long do you hold the note?

PECK For as long as the phrase is. That gives me the feeling of what it's like to hold one air through the phrase. Then I will play the actual notes, but with the same air that I had when I only held the one note. The air is constant. I don't like to be playing around with the air, puffing here and backing away there.

P.E. It breaks up the line.

PECK Yes, although one does those things for effect sometimes.

P.E. How do you adjust to all the different halls you play in throughout the year?

PECK You learn by doing. It's a matter of experience and each hall is different. It's really not fair to judge an orchestra in a strange hall.

P.E. Do you live music?

PECK I live my life, and music is the major part of my life. How terrible it would be if there were no music. I am sometimes sad that I know the orchestral repertoire so well. I remember the first time I heard *Death and Transfiguration* of Richard Strauss. It was so marvelous. It's not that I don't enjoy the orchestral music anymore. What I'm saying is that there are few new pieces for me to discover. Therefore, I am branching out into the opera repertoire through performances and recordings. Music is a disease that we all have and we can't get away from it. There is no cure. But who wants to be cured? I am happy that I appreciate and enjoy music, and I want to play it as beautifully and honestly as I can.

JAMES PAPPOUTSAKIS

JAMES PAPPOUTSAKIS

Born in Cairo of Greek parents, Mr. Pappoutsakis came to America as a boy. He was educated at the Boston Latin School and the New England Conservatory of Music where he studied with Georges Laurent.

In 1937, he joined the Boston Symphony as assistant principal flute and the Boston Pops as principal flute. He has toured Japan and Australia with the Boston Symphony as first flutist with Charles Munch conducting, and was the soloist with the Zimbler Sinfonietta on their tour to Central and South America. In 1960 and 1968, he played concertos by Telemann and Bach with the Symphony in Boston and at the Berkshire Festival, as well as many appearances with the Boston Pops Orchestra, Arthur Fiedler conducting.

Mr. Pappoutsakis is on the faculty of the New England Conservatory, Boston University and the Longy School. He began teaching in 1942 and has taught many Fulbright winners.

He is married and has a daughter. His wife was the harpist with the Boston Symphony Orchestra under Serge Koussevitzky.

SETTING

Mr. Pappoutsakis had emerged from a long rehearsal with the Boston Symphony Orchestra as I arrived to interview him in his studio at the New England Conservatory of Music. "Let me catch my breath," he said, sitting down and touching his brow with a white linen handkerchief. Slightly weary, but with his spirited enthusiasm lighting his kind face, he smiled, saying, "Next come my students." His studio has just the essentials: a piano, chairs, music stands and is well lighted.

Dapper and elegant in a dark blue suit, blue and white pin stripe shirt, red tie and navy blue silk stockings, his abundant silver white hair and moustache exquisitely groomed, his nails polished, he impressed one with his air of discriminate refinement. An aristocrat — seemingly agreeable to a more tranquil ambience than that of harrying symphonic schedules and rehearsals.

Mr. Pappoutsakis's manner was informal and spontaneous, though conservative. His warm voice, gliding gently, was traced with an undercurrent of intensity. Busy but not harried, he said, "I am enjoying myself with all of this!"

INTERVIEW

P.E. You studied with Georges Laurent, who was the epitome of the French school. Are there still distinct schools of flute playing?

PAPPOUTSAKIS. Not so much nowadays. I don't think you could draw the line . . . perhaps a little bit with the German school, but there is no real difference. It has evened out. I mean, there are natural, personal differences. As a matter of fact, I think American flute players can hold their own against anybody nowadays.

P.E. How did this evening out happen?

PAPPOUTSAKIS. First of all, you take the teachers of sixty or fifty years ago. There was George Barrère, Laurent, Moyse, who in turn brought about Kincaid and those of us in the symphonies now. We all stem from the same tradition and each of us has added his own personality. You take Baker — Baker was a pupil of Kincaid and Mariano, who in turn was a pupil of Barrère, and so on.

P.E. Do you find any common problems among your students of college and conservatory level?

PAPPOUTSAKIS. No . . . actually, the level of flute playing across the country has gone up a tremendous, trememdous degree. People are entering the conservatories now using material they used to graduate with playing ten or fifteen years ago. They think nothing of walking in here and playing a Prokofieff sonata or an Ibert concerto from memory right out of high school! I think they are ahead of most other wind instrumentalists. As a matter of fact, it's a standing joke around here that the flute players when they come to audition are so far above any of the other instrumentalists that we sometimes let the other panels, say, for clarinet or bassoon just come and listen.

P.E. To what do you attribute this higher standard among the students now?

PAPPOUTSAKIS. First, the number of players has produced competition. The number of recordings and the repertory for the flute is so far above any other wind instrument.

P.E. Do you mean in quality — in volume?

PAPPOUTSAKIS. In quality *and* in volume. You take the trombone or the clarinet: they have no Baroque music to speak of, and again, there is a tremendous amount of recordings so flutists have the sound in their ears from an early age. I remember in my day there were very few recordings — just a handful! This is about forty years ago, but now, my goodness there are millions of them!

P.E. When did the standards begin changing?

PAPPOUTSAKIS. It's been a gradual process, but I'd say in the last ten or fifteen years. Well, now, the problem is this: there are so many good players, I'm speaking of the high school level, that this has brought about some good and some bad things. For example, we have here, at the Boston Conservatory, let's say, some

thirty-two or thirty-five flute players. At Indiana University, I think it's something like seventy-five or eighty flute players. At Manhattan — well, you could go right down the line — every school has thirty or forty. So the results are that it's hard to get orchestra or chamber experience because you don't have thirty-two flutes in the orchestra. On the other hand, it's wonderful because some of my students, before they even graduate, have twenty or twenty-five pupils apiece — just young kids who take lessons. So when they do graduate, even though they may not get a postion playing, they certainly can make an excellent living, whereas a bassoon player, unless he is of the caliber to get a good position, well, he's going to have it a little rough . . .there aren't enough bassoon pupils like there are for the flute.

P.E. Do you find any differences in musical development and taste between college and conservatory students?

PAPPOUTSAKIS I'll get to your question, but first, let me say that I've had now about seventeen Fulbright winners and the numbers are just about equally divided between those of the Conservatory or those of the liberal arts college. I've had them from Brandeis, Harvard, Radcliffe, as well as the Boston Conservatory, so, as far as the level of flute playing is concerned — it's about the same, but you'll find, for example, the students at Brandeis or Harvard, are apt to be very, very sophisticated . . . just a touch snobbish.

P.E. In what way?

PAPPOUTSAKIS You know, in teaching the flute there are certain pieces that you give — not from the point of the merit of the piece but from the point of what is happening to the person as a flute player. There is a whole repertory of French pieces from the Paris Conservatory, it's junk frankly — it's not good music, but what is important is what it makes a flute player do . . . inflections, changes of color. It's a medium. But if you try to give this to someone sophisticated, he'll say, "Don't you have something else? Don't you have something else that'll bring about the same results?" Whereas the conservatory students seem to be more down to earth. They figure, "Look, this is a profession — you have to do this and that." These differences have to do with being exposed to the more avant garde, to more areas of art, whereas in the conservatory it's strictly music.

P.E. Do you favor the strict music background offered in the conservatory?

PAPPOUTSAKIS Yes and no. There are just about as many good ones coming out of both. Look, don't forget that as far as an instrument is concerned, the main thing is talent and the amount of time that's put into it, and although, I suppose, over the long run it does reflect if one has read a great deal of philosophy or whatever, but that doesn't show up quite as much — it's how one plays the instrument that counts. I remember when I first came to the orchestra in 1937, there was a period right before the season started and I thought, "Gee, I'm going to be with all those great musicians! I'd better start reading up on composers' lives and biographies of musicians." But when I got there, they were talking about who was going to play poker! Of course, it has changed a great deal since, so that they are better educated, but you found that the French musicians had taken up their instrument at a very early age—almost to the exclusion of all other forms of education—but they were very good! Oh, my gosh, to hear some of those Frenchmen solfege something—was fantastic!

P.E. When did you begin your apprenticeship?

PAPPOUTSAKIS Oh, I guess it was when I was very little. I came to America from Egypt when I was five or six. Actually, it was my brother who played the viola and I was looking for something to do and I was just attracted by it, but not by having heard it but by the looks of the instrument—isn't that silly!

P.E. Did it look easy to play?

PAPPOUTSAKIS Well, the flute does have the advantage that it sounds good in the early stages—not like the violin or the clarinet. So, if you have a little ego about it, you can say, "Heh, listen to me producing these sounds." I think that's one of the reasons it has attracted so many youngsters—you get encouraged . . . at the beginning.

P.E. How long have you been teaching now?

PAPPOUTSAKIS Oh, if you want to date me! But that's silly. I'd say since 1942 or 1943. A good thirty years.

P.E. Do you stress the same areas in your teaching or has your approach changed?

PAPPOUTSAKIS We all learn. When I first started, I had very young students. I don't have the same problem now but I used to go about it a little too strictly and too seriously. Now I'd never be like that. Once I had a twelve year old youngster and the parent came to me and said, "Look, I want my youngster to think back to her youth with pleasure. Don't spoil it for her." But, I don't think I've changed. We are apt to put into our teaching what we felt we should have had—it's like the parent who feels that their parents were strict so they'll be lenient or the reverse.

P.E. What were your lessons with Georges Laurent like?

PAPPOUTSAKIS He was a tremendous player! A very kind man. He did very little analyzing and very little explanation. The procedure would be this—you'd go in; he'd greet you and it was always formal, never by the first name or anything like that, and you would begin by playing four pages of scales, and he'd make some remark such as "Good, but watch the intonation." You'd play a four page Andersen and he'd say, "One mistake is all right but two, you don't know it yet." But at the end of the lesson, he would pick up his flute and play perhaps eight bars or so, and you'd walk out in a trance, it was so gorgeous! So beautiful! Anyway, you went home thinking, "Well, he said the staccato wasn't good but he didn't say whether it was too hard or too soft." You explored and explored until you found it. As a result, I went the other way and tried to explain what the tongue does

and, Oh!, at that time, when I studied, a student was afraid to ask questions for fear that he would be thought of as being without talent. Then they'd say, "Oh, if you want to analyze that much, perhaps you should be doing something else." I mean, if you asked what the tongue did or about the column of air, they'd say, "Perhaps you don't have natural talent." But since then, we've gone into a great deal of analysis—sometimes I wonder if it isn't too much. I once had a student who'd just come out of the army and I suppose it was understandable . . . but he had a checklist of questions and he said, "Before we go any further I have a few questions! When you stop a note do you stop from the diaphragm or the throat? Now, what does the tongue do?" After awhile, I felt I was against the ropes!

P.E. Calling for time.

PAPPOUTSAKIS Right! But now I don't have too much of that. As I said, the greatest thing is the fact that they have something to listen to through recordings and live concerts. So, their concept of tone is so good that very few people have a poor tone.

P.E. What do you try to impress most upon your students about playing?

PAPPOUTSAKIS As far as the actual playing is concerned, I have always thought that the quality of tone comes first because it's the first thing anyone hears. If the tone isn't interesting, then the people won't listen and explore beyond that.

P.E. If one had to choose between having a fabulous technique or a fabulous tone—which would be a better choice?

PAPPOUTSAKIS If someone had such a technique, let's say, it wouldn't manifest itself in a competition because if there were two flute players, the final two to be chosen, the one with the better technical ability probably wouldn't show up, whereas the tone quality is instantaneous—they'd say, "This one sounds better."

P.E. It must be difficult to have a student who is not too well equipped or who doesn't work. What is the role of the teacher then?

PAPPOUTSAKIS The screening process at a conservatory is so careful and good that you don't find such a situation. Though sometimes, a person may have the equipment, but because of psychological or other reasons, things fall apart. But very few, once they have been admitted, especially since the flute is such a highly competitive instrument, are not equipped to go through it—if they work! If they don't work, of course, all the talent in the world won't save them. But given the talent and the desire to work, it usually works out. Now, don't forget, some of the students are in music education so they don't really have to be such fine performers—even though many of them are.

P.E. Can you tell right away if someone is talented?

PAPPOUTSAKIS I think talent manifests itself in many ways. After all, if a person doesn't have talent, chances are he would not continue with the instrument.

You take, for instance, the number of kids who are made to take piano lessons—very few continue. But if a kid has talent, first of all, he'll have a tremendous interest and his ego would be built up by the fact that he sounds good.

P.E. You've mentioned ego a few times. Does one play out of ego? How much does it have to do with being a good musician?

PAPPOUTSAKIS A performer has to have it. You could call it ego or you could call it self respect. But a performer has to have a certain amount of it—it's necessary to have self esteem; to have the confidence that what you're doing is good. A musician has to be out there in person to present his wares and you need that confidence—that feeling that you've worked hard and that you've got something worthwhile to present. You know, there are many players who sound beautiful backstage but cannot do very well in public. You have to be able to face the music.

P.E. What do you think are the qualities that signal out a first class flutist?

PAPPOUTSAKIS Sensitivity and imagination. First of all, since the flute is somewhat limited as far as dynamic range is concerned, you therefore have to make up for that with inflections and imagination. It takes every bit of subtlety and imagination to make a full length flute recital interesting.

P.E. When you first begin teaching someone, what do you look for in particular?

PAPPOUTSAKIS Right now, I'm impressed with someone who has a natural sense of style—who has the ability to hear himself objectively with someone else's ears because, for me, that's the basis of fine playing. It's very easy to sit here and say, "Well, that's out of tune and you aren't making the inflections." But it's the person who hears himself, as others do, who is far ahead of the game. In much the same way that an artist has a discerning eye for color, a musician has to have a high sense of tonal discrimination. Let me tell you an anecdote: some ten or fifteen years ago, there was this charming southern girl and at that time the school was very uncertain about admitting her, but they said, "Take her, but you'll have to start from the beginning." So, when this young lady came for her first lesson, I was stupid enough to say, "Well, we'll have to start from the beginning." Of course, this offended her. Anyway, she began playing a Handel sonata—it was something unbelievably bad. The tone was terrible! So, again, very stupidly I said, "Let me play it for you." When I finished, she said, "I can't say I hear any appreciable difference." I don't know whether she didn't have a sense of tone, said it to get even, or whether it was not one of my better days.

P.E. How do you go about projecting to your students the difference in musical styles?

PAPPOUTSAKIS Many things contribute to it. First, I do a lot of demonstrating—not that I think I'm that great, but it helps. Secondly, when they're as interested as they are, they attend concerts, they have record-ings . . . all the differences of style you learn through listening.

P.E. Do you have a special method for helping with technique?

PAPPOUTSAKIS I try to think of it in a very logical way, whether that's due to my Greek background or square mind, I don't know. I break it down in terms of parts of the body, so I say, let's exclude all imagination and just use our tools; the fingers, lips, tongue; breathing apparatus. I give exercises that are very simple but are effective, that strengthen the fingers and make the tongue agile. I try to pin down what each player's weakness is and you'll find it's either these two fingers or those two. So the exercises become a sort of checklist for them—everyday they check the lips, fingers, tongue and breath control. Now, it's not that these exercises are going to cure anything but they're indicators—an indication of what's beginning to deteriorate.

P.E. If a student asks you if he has the "tone"—if he's got the "right tone," what do you say?

PAPPOUTSAKIS Ah, tone is a conception. You can't really teach tone or describe it because it's the character—the person speaking—his personality and that's crucial to a player—to a performer.

P.E. How do you manage to do so much? You have the Pops, the Symphony, your teaching . . .

PAPPOUTSAKIS I just fill in the hours every day with about six hours of teaching or sometimes seven—I even teach Sundays. As a matter of fact, I leave the house in the morning about ten and come home about ten o'clock at night. And there are always concerts on Tuesdays, Thursdays, Fridays and Saturdays—also on Wednesdays there are usually two rehearsals. Once the season starts, there is no break for me until the end of August.

P.E. Is that when your summer at Tanglewood ends?

PAPPOUTSAKIS Yes. I enjoy all of this! You know why? Because no two people are alike—no two people have the same personality. At the beginning of the year, I look and I dread the idea of forty or fifty students . . . then each one comes in with their aliveness, their personality—and starry eyed! It's not like an eight hour job.

P.E. Music is your life.

PAPPOUTSAKIS Yes! That's all. I have no other interests of any kind.

P.E. You've been playing in the Symphony and the Pops for about thirty-five years now. Has the makeup of the orchestra changed much?

PAPPOUTSAKIS In the makeup of the orchestra there have been a lot of changes. I think it's a younger orchestra where before it was mostly Europeans. For example, when I came in 1937 there were only three or four Americans—trained musicians and most of them older people. There was a great deal of formality. You'd go in and shake hands with practically everyone. Now, you never think of going into rehearsal with a formal jacket and tie—you go in with jeans and things like that.

P.E. Have the demands of playing in the orchestra changed?

PAPPOUTSAKIS No . . . no, it's still a five rehearsal week. What has changed and has increased are the number of performances. When I first began, there was a Friday and Saturday concert, and perhaps six Tuesday afternoons and six Sundays but now we play every Tuesday, Thursday, Friday and Saturday. There are four concerts a week whereas before there were only two.

P.E. Did this increase in performances come about because of greater public interest?

PAPPOUTSAKIS Because of the musicians' demands and rightfully so! The demands kept going up because they wanted a better salary and the one way they could get it was to provide more music.

P.E. So more and different skills were demanded from the musicians too?

PAPPOUTSAKIS Yes . . . now, I'm speaking not so much for myself but for the younger musicians. They can interpret a wider variety of music—avant garde, classics, because their training has been broader than ours. Take for example, the range of the instrument: my teacher would never let us practice above high B or C. They thought that would strain the lips or they told us to avoid flutter tonguing but now all of that has changed.

P.E. Speaking of changes, I understand that when Lucas Foss's piece *Time Cycle* was played, members of the Symphony weren't too receptive to it. Why was that?

PAPPOUTSAKIS Well, I think I can explain. A musician who has spent his lifetime perfecting his tone quality and his technique resents having to play anything where these qualities are abused and where in effect, it's said to him, "Well, I don't care if you have a beautiful tone—I want you to sound like a fog horn," or when conductors or composers come to us and we play . . . and they say, "Oh, no! No! It must sound as if you're retching." What are you going to tell them? I haven't spent thirty years of my life—nobody has—to sound like that! It is almost a sadistic thing. It's almost as if you were asking a doctor to come to your house, who has every expectation of doing his work, and you say, "Oh, no, I want you to scrub the floors." Well, he'd say, "Get someone whose job it is to scrub floors!" This is why the musicians resent the fact that they're asked to do things that aren't in the scheme of things when they took up the instrument.

P.E. But don't you feel the composer should still challenge the musician?

PAPPOUTSAKIS Yes, exactly. I do think a lot of modern music is absolutely terrific. But the good composers do not abuse the instrument nor make a degenerate of the player—what I mean is, they don't offend him. Look, I have absolutely the greatest respect for any exploration but with one reservation: no abuse to the instrument and musician. I like to think that there is a partnership—a fifty-fifty partnership between composer and player-performer, in the sense that sometimes a player may play something beyond the wildest expectations of a composer—whether it's Bach or Beethoven. I think the time has come for a new and natural exploration, an extension of the flute, but within musical boundaries.

P.E. What do you think of the musical period we are in right now?

PAPPOUTSAKIS I think a lot of the music being written is too contrived and too clever—too gimmicky. Many times, it's a bore because it requires too much explanation. Who needs it? Music should be immediate enjoyment and not require a blue print to be enjoyed.

P.E. What are the basic skills needed to play in an orchestra, chamber group and as a soloist?

PAPPOUTSAKIS For an orchestra, flexibility. That he or she be able to give the conductor what he wants—that is a wonderful asset. After all, although there is a certain amount of individual interpretation in a particular solo, you are under the direction of someone who makes the decisions and you should be able to communicate what he wants. You should have flexibility in all areas.

P.E. And what are the skills that chamber playing demands?

PAPPOUTSAKIS They are very specialized, very refined, and distinct. A chamber group demands a distilled kind of playing. It takes a great deal of playing together—a quartet will practice two years or more almost daily and still not reach the superb perfection that would be considered first class. Now, a soloist . . . this may sound terrible but a soloist has to have a touch of the ham actor in him. I once knew a cellist who I thought was the greatest cellist in the world—I still have a great respect for him. I said, "Mr Bedetti I think you're the greatest cellist in the world." And he said, "No . . . no." "Well, then the second greatest." He said, "That, I will accept." And Koussevisky would say to him, "Mr. Bedetti, that's an extremely difficult passage for the cello." He would say, "For the section, perhaps, but not for a Bedetti." He had this supreme confidence but it wasn't offensive because it was so . . . real and so genuine.

P.E. Do you have any special method for memorizing a piece?

PAPPOUTSAKIS I always suggest that you repeat things many times in the early stages in order to get them under your fingers or it's just as easy, when trying to get over a difficult passage, of let's say two bars, to walk away from the music on the fourth or fifth try and play it. Memorizing is an accumulative process and pretty soon you've a string of lines that you put together.

P.E. How can you get the most out of practicing?

PAPPOUTSAKIS You must focus on the point where the trouble is. You'll find someone going over and over an eight bar phrase when the stumbling block is a particular interval. So, they're playing thirty-two notes when they need only play two. The other thing is to determine whether the difficulty is of the eye or of the technique. Many years ago, when I was "up and at 'em," I had a tape recorder and I'd say to the student, "Now, play me the most fantastic, the most difficult passage you could think of." Then, with the help of my brother, who has very wonderful ears, he's professor of music at the University of Vermont, we then slowed the thing down and wrote it out. Oh, there would be groups of seventeen notes, stacatto, legato ... and six months later I'd show it to the student and ask him to play it. Well, he'd say, "I can't possibly play that!" You see, when learning something I try to tell them, if it's a question of the eye not absorbing the picture, it has to be in a sense very much like a time exposure on a camera when the subject is in the dark. In other words, you have to have more time to absorb the picture. You have to practice something so very slowly, that the picture, the image in your eye is developed. Otherwise, they'll never know what is wrong—whether it's the finger technique or what. It won't be logically figured out.

P.E. Have your own methods of practice changed over the years?

PAPPOUTSAKIS I do the same things within reason. I think all our teaching is an offshoot of our own methods. I try, but I can't say that now I have as much time to practice, but I think that I play, perhaps, more maturely than I used to. I don't think I could improve my tone at this late date or improve my technique—it is, what it is now, but I try to think of using it more intelligently.

P.E. Can a teacher help a student aspire to be an artist?

PAPPOUTSAKIS I most certainly do. I think that one of the fundamental roles of a teacher is not only to maintain interest but to inspire, and with each student it's an entirely different approach. With one you may do it by praise, with another one, by criticism—but you have to find what will do it for each person.

P.E. What are you looking forward to now?

PAPPOUTSAKIS To continue playing and teaching as long as I feel I have something to contribute in these areas—I'm enjoying myself with all of this!

EUGENIA ZUKERMAN

EUGENIA ZUKERMAN

Since her highly acclaimed debut in New York in 1971, Eugenia Zukerman has been acclaimed as one of the finest flutists to be found anywhere. A graduate of the Juilliard School, she has concertized extensively throughout North America, Europe and Israel. An unusually versatile artist, she appears not only in recital and as soloist with orchestra, but with many chamber music societies as well. Together with the classical pianist Carlos Bonell, Eugenia Zukerman has formed a new duo, performing primarily works of the Baroque period. Eugenia Zukerman also performs in joint recital with her husband, violinist, Pinchas Zukerman.

"Few flutists have staged as enjoyable a recital as Mrs. Zukerman. The secret lies in her musicianship, which is consummate, and her taste, which is immaculate, and her stage presence — she is a sheer pleasure to watch."

The New York Times

"Mrs. Zukerman's tone is light, bright and bird-like. When this was added to the beauty of Mrs. Zukerman and the sheer grace with which she played the flute, few could have escaped her spell."

The New York Post

SETTING

"I'm pulling strings but it probably won't do any good. We're trying to get a visa for the nanny—she's crucial to our existence." She smiles, greeting me; her handshake is strong and direct but her face looks worried. "Pinky and the children left for London this morning," she says showing me into the living room and apologizing and excusing herself to make another call. Elegant. Imperious. She strides quickly across the room dressed in a black skirt, black boots and a black and red print blouse with flowing sleeves that move like butterfly wings.

I sat on a sofa and placed my cassette on a brass table top. It was 2 p.m. in New York and the sun lit up the room, the trees on Riverside Drive and the Hudson River below. Reds, blacks, oranges, blues and golds warmed and dramatized the room. There were sofas, chairs, a metronome on a marble table top, film cans ("from photographs taken this morning,") music and books on the coffee table: *The Final Diary* by Ned Rorem, biographies of Liszt and Beethoven, ivy plants, oil paintings and prints, chinese lamps on end tables, a piano by the huge window and behind me in the dining room, a bright, red poinsettia.

"I try to do what makes everybody comfortable — it balances the whole but rarely do I feel balanced." She laughs. She is a beauty: Petite, blonde with a high forehead and cheekbones, the mouth full, the skin luminous and large green eyes which are quick to change and although one intuits a whip of temper, an impatience, there is a compassion, a humility and a deep concern for people. Feminine, dainty, yet no flimsy spirit here; hers is the nurturing and pure presence of a stream.

Our conversation lasted two and a half hours and she spoke with enthusiasm and sincerity. She was on guard at the beginning of the interview, touching her pearl earrings and necklace, her bright voice arched, but soon she tucked her legs underneath her, her voice relaxed and one felt at home.

Intelligent, practical, with a passionate reserve, like an empress, but an un-pampered one, for although she has help, she cooks herself and rises at 6 a.m., charting her way through the day and night, overlooking and protecting her family court filled with the brilliance of the world's famous musicians, concert halls, cities and with schedules and surprises to handle, the apartment in New York, the flat in London, touring, performing, recording, practicing, travelling with her famous husband, taking care of crying children in planes and airports and during a blackout in Israel, holding an infant while bombs exploded in Damascus. Through this all, she is intent on her solo career. Guiding her own world apart: her music, her writing. "My life is like a Chinese menu. Life is very, very full."

INTERVIEW

P.E. Did you think about the Mozart Concerti for a long time before recording them?

ZUKERMAN Not really because I had played them quite a bit and I felt ready to record them when it was planned. First of all, I thought, that if I wasn't pleased with them I wouldn't release them and also if I re-recorded them in five years time, I would be free to do that. For myself, it's just a very nice record of the way I'm thinking now. Also, it's a collaboration with Pinky. This record is very interesting to me because I had a very bad back accident. I couldn't stand up because I had pulled out my pelvis and three vertebrae and the pain was just excruciating. The recording took place about four or five weeks after the accident. I was propped up on a stool. I felt miserable as you do when you are in pain and a little bit petulant. I felt what was coming out was absolutely awful — that's the gist of it. Then when I was in Europe in October and the head of CBS said "I want you to come and listen to these tapes and I said, "Yes, I know it was a wasted session." He said, "You're crazy. It's just terrific. We're putting it out right away." So I went there and sure enough there was something that I could live with. It's not my ideal but it's something that I am very happy with. The thing that is interesting is that I thought I had produced nothing.

P.E. When I spoke to Mr. Baker about having to play when not feeling well, he said, "Some days I feel really good and other days I feel I can't play anything. Half the number of days throughout the year I say, "Oh, I really feel like playing. I really should record this — right now! But the strange part of it is that I've recorded when I thought I was terrific — felt terrific and I've listened to the recording one next to the other and I can't tell which day I felt good and when I didn't. It's not even apparent to me! You see art is a state of feeling — not of physical feeling."

ZUKERMAN When you are not feeling well, other areas take over for you. The tension is not centered in the areas of the brain that focus on finger dexterity or tongue production so the pressure is off the areas that you need for good playing. I also felt slightly more confident because it made me think to myself, "I've been playing the flute for twenty years and I do have some kind of solid technique to rely on and solid tone production that will function without my standing there and beating at them." You should never allow yourself to do things automatically but I think it's very hard to be objective about what you are producing.

P.E. On the Mozart recording you collaborated with Pinky. Are your musical ideas similar and what have you learned?

ZUKERMAN I think his ideas about Mozart are just ideal. I've learned more from Pinky than I've learned from anyone. In a musical sense and also in the sense of sound production. His is a most beautiful, ravishing sound. The way that he approaches music is just very catching.

P.E. What did you learn about sound production?

ZUKERMAN I learned about centering the sound. Focusing. I learned about it in a different vocabulary than I did from wind players. A string player won't talk about "spinning" or "focusing" the sound. The terms are slightly different and also the sound is different. I learned about tone production in the sense of never playing a "white note." I try for constant vibration, constant intensity and a lot of attention to phrasing and the overall view.

P.E. The architecture.

ZUKERMAN Absolutely. Also, the ability to sustain. One of the gorgeous things about a beautiful violin line is that there is never a break and it should be the same in flute playing.

P.E. What do you do technically to achieve this unbroken line?

ZUKERMAN Technically I have practiced playing very long phrases.

P.E. Long tones and what specific phrases?

ZUKERMAN Long tones and phrases that demand a great deal of sustaining breath control like the opening of *Afternoon of a Faun* or *Syrinx*. You have to practice these things musically because just holding your breath for three minutes is one thing but to be able to play one beautiful phrase is another thing. You have to be able to think while playing at the beginning and end of a phrase in order to make that long arch. To take flight all the time.

P.E. How do you manage to take flight?

ZUKERMAN I think I actually hear certain harmonic pinpoints within the phrase. This is something I learned from Pinky and also because I play the piano — not well — but melodic single line instruments tend to get very involved in the instrument and not in the listening to the music vertically as well as horizontally. I try to listen to it vertically and that helps the shape of a phrase. I will think to myself of key words like flowing, floating or spinning the sound and feeling it vibrating.

P.E. I am very impressed by your clarity and articulation.

ZUKERMAN That's good!

P.E. Before recording the Mozart Concerti and the Andante, how did you analyze the pieces and think about shaping them? It is such a great venture to record them.

ZUKERMAN It was gutsy. Yet, on the other hand, it's one of the things that you live with your whole life as a flutist. I played the D major when I was sixteen with the Hartford Symphony — some prize winning thing so I was very comfortable with the D major. But the G major, although I had practiced it, I had never played it in public until 1971 in some castle in Scotland. I haven't played them all that much, so in no way am I tired of them. But style wise I have listened to a lot of people play Mozart. Pinky's Mozart in particular helps me because he manages to have enormous energy and at the same time great virility and great depth. He produces a sort of ease. It's not mannered. I had played the Mozart concerti for him. I had performed the C major Andante in recital and that took a lot of thinking about. In the concerti, the long phrases are straight forward rondo allegro forms and I am aware of when the development happens. I have analyzed them musicalogically and then I have analyzed them in terms of mood. For example, the opening of the G major is very majestic and very grand. It has to be gracious. It's elegant and I think that the last movement is very bravura and the slow movement of each of them are just marvelous, singing cantabile movements whereas the opening movement of the D major concerto, I think of as being less on a grand scale but much more perky and real brillo kind of writing. The first movement is very witty. Pinky has a very fine idea about the wit of the last movement. If you hold back in certain places, it will emphasize an idea which is clever or adroit.

P.E. Selectivity and understatement.

ZUKERMAN And clarity, which I worked very hard at. I think it is so important that the pieces be impeccable. By no means, are mine. I have heard more perfect ones.

P.E. Which are the most challenging and difficult passages for you in the Mozart?

ZUKERMAN In the D major I find there are some tricky passages that have to do with the fourth finger of the right hand. If I had the score, I could tell you exactly where they are but I always have trouble with the fourth finger of my right hand like everyone does. In the G major you have so many F sharps. In the D major the last movement is particularly hard because it's extremely awkward. It's awkward and one has a terrible tendency to rush it and take it too fast. I don't like to do that.

P.E. What are the traps inherent in the music when playing Mozart?

ZUKERMAN You can rush. You can lose scope. In the first movement of the G Major, it's such a grand piece, such a grand movement but you have to have a real thrust through the entire movement. That's one movement I'm not happy with on the recording because I don't think it has that kind of thrust that a performance would have. I think, to get back to problems, the D major and the G major — both of those slow movements are very, very hard to sustain. It takes a great deal of work.

P.E. Have you ever done circular breathing?

ZUKERMAN No, I've tried it but I didn't get anywhere with it. I have tried in my studies to try out tricky things like I'd sing various exercises for breathing making sure that I breathed deeply. I did have to work on not breathing over the larynx. I had a tendency to "ugh!," everytime I inhaled. A lot of flutists have this. It's very hard not to hear breathing sounds, but I'm better at that now. It is part of natural breathing because if you are natural and relaxed and your throat is opened, the air you take in won't make a noise. I have come to think of breathing as being very, very natural. You have to be able to expand your capacity especially at the back of the lungs.

P.E. Have you done yoga or other exercise?

ZUKERMAN I haven't done yoga but I have danced and I've had two children with natural childbirth with no problems. I just gave two pushes and each of them were born and I had absolutely no problem with hyperventilating or the breathing. That's important during pregnancy and I am sure it's because of the flute playing.

P.E. I've listened to your recording of the three Bachs with Rampal and your husband. What are the technical and style differences between the Bachs and Mozart?

ZUKERMAN To go backwards from Mozart, J. C. Bach was very near to Mozart, of course, in timing and also in feeling — the kind of very early Mozart in feeling. But it's much less multi-level, there is much less going on. It is more straight forward but it is very early classical. You can't see him as baroque but to go back to W. F. Ernst Bach which is for two flutes and viola, a trio, it is very high baroque. In playing one wants a less bravura sound, but first of all, you're talking about solo and chamber music which are two very different things. Playing with Rampal, we were all listening very carefully and all blending very carefully. The Mozart is an enlarged idea of chamber music.

P.E. How did you cultivate your ability to listen?

ZUKERMAN I realized that listening is very important. Listening to the notes with an intelligent approach to what one hears.

P.E. A responsible approach.

ZUKERMAN Responsible and a response to.

P.E. How did your students help you to become a responsible listener?

ZUKERMAN That's a good question. The playing in itself. In playing and stopping and asking myself, "What do I hear?" When you are working on things, to stop and work on intonations — to be listening from that point of view. At Juilliard, when I played in the orchestra, I would very much try to make myself concentrate on the solo part I was playing but also to what was going on all around me. It takes a certain amount of security to do that. It's like tight rope walking. If you can tight rope walk and look up then you are free. It's hard to define awareness. As you get older and mature, you are able to take in many more things into your perspective. As a child, you may be in a room filled with people but you will only notice how *you* feel or only that *you* want a piece of chocolate cake; but when you are an adult, you will notice someone's clothing or someone seems unhappy over there or someone is laughing over there. Your senses are more widely opened and it's the same thing in music. You have to allow the whole musical experience to feed you.

P.E. Were you encouraged to play the flute as a child?

ZUKERMAN I played the piano. My mother was a dancer and my father was a scientist but he sang and I had an older sister who was very gifted at the piano and I was looking for a second instrument. There was a demonstration of instruments at my grammar school and I heard the flute and I was just enchanted. I found out that I could study it and I was able to do it through the public school system.

P.E. Where?

ZUKERMAN In West Hartford, Connecticut. I studied it through high school but I was not sure whether I wanted to be a professional. I had a few lessons with Pappoutsakis in Boston. Then I went to Barnard College where I studied for two years but after two years of Barnard I decided to go professionally into music so I switched to Juilliard. I had planned to have an orchestral career. I think that you have to be realistic. One does not pick up the flute, at least not in my day, perhaps things have changed, but you didn't take the flute in order to be a virtuoso. You could do your chasing of the red herring but you have to be realistic.

P.E. I don't think it's changed.

ZUKERMAN I was first flutist of the Juilliard Orchestra and I felt this was what I could do. I was going to go out to Denver but then Pinky and I decided to get married. I began travelling with him and we would play chamber music along the way but I didn't know quite what to do so I entered the Young Concert Artists Competition in 1971 and I won it. It gave me my very first recital. I got really terrific reviews which was a marvelous morale booster and this started me to get organized and it also gave me a management — the Young Concert Artists. They started to book me for concerts. It all began very gradually and it wasn't until I had my first child that I became very busy. It's a funny way to go about things. It's hard with children but the solo playing just evolved.

P.E. What influences or change in yourself made you decide to go into music professionally?

ZUKERMAN I had planned to write and I am still doing it but I felt that I had a couple of areas in which I was gifted. I am not academic and I was not interested in going into a heavy academic career like getting a masters degree or Ph.D. in order to write or teach writing. Music had always intrigued me and I thought that I could have a nice combination of things if I were to be able to teach music, as well as play, and that would probably leave me enough time to do some writing. As it turned out, with travelling with Pinky and the hecticness of our lives, I didn't start writing again until two years ago.

P.E. How was your experience at Juilliard different from Barnard College?

ZUKERMAN It was a big contrast because at Barnard there are people bumping around saying, "This year I think I'll study geometry or next year maybe anthropology." They have no sense of urgency. But when you get to Juilliard, there are these eighteen year old kids who are thirty-five in their outlook. They have one goal. They are very driven. They are tremendously motivated. It's the world of people who know what they want and what they want to do.

P.E. Where did you feel most comfortable?

ZUKERMAN I felt like an outsider at Juilliard. I have a lot of interests and I am not just driven to play music but that was allright because I had a life outside of Juilliard. I was involved in the Columbia scene. Musically, at Juilliard, it was at a very high level and at Columbia they had an orchestra and they had music courses but it was very dilettantish. It was very competitive at Juilliard.

P.E. How did you get to be first flutist in the Juilliard Orchestra?

ZUKERMAN It was luck. If you are auditioning for an orchestra, you look at orchestral excerpts. I studied orchestral excerpts and I would listen to the whole piece so I would have an idea of context. I just studied the excerpts like the forty other flutists. For some reason, when it came to my turn and the conductor pointed to *Afternoon of a Faun* or Brahms' *First*, I played it and he liked it. That's luck. I am sure there were an awful lot of fine flutists like Ann Denier, who is now first in Los Angeles, Jeanne Baxtresser, who is first in Montreal, Scott Groff, who is playing somewhere — so many of them who went on to really stellar careers as orchestral musicians. I prepared for the audition by diligently practicing the orchestral excerpts — just doing what you have to do.

P.E. How did you prepare for the Young Artists Competition?

ZUKERMAN I was very relaxed about it. I chose pieces that I liked very much and that I knew I played very well. I know the kinds of music that I play best. I chose the pieces that I was comfortable with. I think being relaxed was very useful.

P.E. How do you help yourself to be relaxed?

ZUKERMAN I try to be relaxed in everything. My life is very complicated — with the children, organizing this and that and the travelling — one has to be able to block out one's extraneous problems. One has to try to think big. It's hard to but that's what I try to do. As far as relaxing is concerned living with Pinky is a great help because he is very relaxed and very natural. His whole approach to music is devoid of neurosis.

P.E. He doesn't become nervous before a performance? You don't clash at certain times?

ZUKERMAN To risk sounding like a Pollyanna, we don't clash. We are both very strong personalities so it's not like we're milquetoasts hanging around each other. If I get angry at him, I will tell him what it's about. We never seem to have angry blow ups. I think that if you are going to be playing music together there is a natural tendency to want to communicate with each other. It's been hard for me because he is so relaxed. He doesn't demand from me that I be as he is. But he sets this great example of being relaxed and confident — that he is going to play the best that he can play. In a way it's like playing with a better player — it gets you up, it makes you feel you could do it, it makes you feel you want to, it makes you feel you won't make mistakes ... it makes you really excited. I got the same feeling when I worked with Rampal. He has the same kind of buoyancy that

Pinky has. He eggs you on to play and his confidence keeps yours buoyant.

P.E. From what source do you think Pinky's confidence stems from?

ZUKERMAN Several things. It comes from a good and very core feeling about himself as a person. As a mother, that's something I deal with all the time—how to make the children feel terrific about themselves. How to have a sense of self. Second of all, to have the knowledge to know what you can do. Obviously, Pinky knows he is gifted but he doesn't use this in any malicious kind of way. It's a fact, like I have green eyes and blonde hair. The confidence also comes from experience. He was confident when we met and he was eighteen and he didn't have experience. He simply knew what to do. He knew he belonged on the stage. He wasn't competitive. It's important to be only competitive with yourself. One of the reasons I enjoyed Juilliard was because I was on the periphery. I was not involved in the politics that went on because I wasn't involved much with the school but I was able to observe what was going on and there was a lot of "She can't play that," or "He can't play that," or "I'm going to play it better than so and so." People get lost and mired down in that. Confidence comes from not dissipating your energies. Being able to focus yourself on what you can do. This is true of everything you do.

P.E. Did you have any difficulty with your breathing when recording the Mozart?

ZUKERMAN There is one phrase, I think, in the G Major that seems to go on and on and on and if you don't get to the bottom of your breath there—you won't get through it. But there are other places where you will want a break before you get to the base of your breathing. I think it must be natural — a flow and ebb. I have noticed with myself, when I am nervous, that it is better for me to concentrate on exhaling. When you are nervous you tend to inhale quite a lot and that can make you dizzy.

P.E. How do you handle the pressure when recording?

ZUKERMAN In recordings I tend to be very concentrated. I like to play through the piece. I don't like starts and stops. I like to get a few master tapes and then I rely on the engineer to tell me and I know myself too which areas need to be redone.

P.E. What other exercises besides the long tones do you like to do?

ZUKERMAN I like to do Taffanel and Gaubert. I like to do some scale work. There are certain things I learned from Baker. He was wonderful. Baker teaches by example very much. I think there is a lot to be said for that. I think it makes you think for yourself — it makes you figure out a great deal. He gives you a firm foundation. We had to do a lot of exercises each week — a lot of études and there were certain exercises that you had to memorize. From Baker I had a very solid idea of tone production and technique.

P.E. How did he help you to focus your sound?

ZUKERMAN It took a long time. Nobody has the sound Julie Baker has. It is so beautiful and bell-like. He would show you how he had his mouth and how he changed the musculature and we would copy it. You could talk about tone production until the cows come home, but you actually have to *do* it. You have to hear. I think a fine example is very important. That is half of it.

P.E. Who have you listened to?

ZUKERMAN Pinky all the time and I listen to singers — I particularly like Janet Baker and Fischer-Dieskau.

P.E. What did you listen for?

ZUKERMAN I listen to how musical they are. How they shape the phrases and make sense out of the music. A singing quality is very important for the flute. You hear it in the voice and the violin. Pinky's sound is just so gorgeous. It's so shimmering and vibrant. As an example, it makes me try to produce the same. You reach different levels at different times. I know that for myself, after my second child was born, I had to play in a *Mostly Mozart Festival* and I hadn't really played much the two months before. I was in lousy shape but I never felt better about my life, family and myself — somehow I feel that my playing only then really reached a level that I was happy with. It's a combination of hard work and perhaps the process of maturity.

P.E. Of living.

ZUKERMAN Yes — experience is one thing but it's also vision.

P.E. Can vision be taught?

ZUKERMAN If you were to take a child from the ghetto and stand him in front of Monet's *WATER LILIES*, you might not reach that one child because he might not have the sensitivity. But you can teach vision. Being exposed to things is crucial. I have been extremely fortunate. We have been able to travel, meet great musicians and play with great musicians.

P.E. What has struck you about these great musicians? Their simplicity?

ZUKERMAN I agree with that — that's true. It has to do with this ability to think on a large scale which enables you to relax. I think of getting to know Arthur Rubenstein and his endless enthusiasm—which he still has and he is going on ninety. That kind of buoyancy and positive quality. He has a very probing mind and is constantly educating himself and is interested in a million things—not just music. That is why his music-making is of a very high order.

P.E. You can't *just* be interested in music — to play music?

ZUKERMAN If you are, then your music is on a smaller level. It doesn't matter what kind of musician you are. You must try to deepen your ability and to appreciate other people's music making. To constantly learn. Last summer Rubenstein was having trouble with his eyes and he was very, very frail and it was during this awful heat-wave in Paris and Pinky was playing Berg's *Kammer-Konzerte* which is for piano, violin and orchestra. It is very esoteric and hard to listen to for anyone. We were having lunch at Rubenstein's and Pinky said he was performing the Berg as well as the Berlioz *Harold in Italy* (on viola) and Rubenstein said, "I am coming! I am coming!" The concert was in the lecture hall of the Paris University. It was one of those nights when you couldn't breathe and I saw him during the intermission and he was absolutely taken with the music. He said, "I want to hear the Berg again. It's the first time I heard it. It's fascinating." He's a man in his nineties — he's just incredible and that is tremendously inspiring.

P.E. How does knowing Arthur Rubenstein inspire you?

ZUKERMAN His enthusiasm and energy inspire me. Knowing someone like Fischer-Dieskau, who is so knowledgeable — it's unbelievable. And Danny Baremboim who also has a great knowledge of music among other things. I've played the Mozart G Major for him. In fact, he wrote some cadenzas for me, some of which I've recorded. He has a very clear idea of style. Nobody could do the certain little things that Danny does in Mozart.

P.E. Have you ever had any conflicts with conductors?

ZUKERMAN No. I don't think there is a problem there. Today music is very open. If there is a disagreement, then I have been able to discuss it openly. I have never worked with a conductor that I didn't enjoy working with. Music making is open. It's no longer this business of the prima donna versus conductor. I have been able to make my point to the conductor and he has been able to make his point.

P.E. Do you work out your ideas about a piece with the conductor beforehand?

ZUKERMAN Often we have a piano rehearsal.

P.E. Could you articulate your ideas about the Mozart?

ZUKERMAN That's difficult and would take time. I am more versed at playing than I am in talking about how I play. It's important to know how you do it, but it's hard to articulate briefly.

P.E. How important was winning the *Young Concert Artists* Competition to your career?

ZUKERMAN It was essential. I didn't know quite how to go about playing. Pinky and I decided very early that he was not going to push people to engage me as well as him. It would have been very easy for him to say, "All-right, I'm playing with the orchestra — can't Genie and I play the *Brandenburg Fifth*?" He felt very strongly that I would resent that . . . after a while. We both agreed that I would have to feel that I was not riding along on his coattails. So he didn't ever ask, "Can Genie play?" I had to find a way to be presented on my own. The *Young Concert Artists* does exactly that — presents you on your own. It probably would have been easier if I'd had a daddy-type of husband who could have said, "I'm going to get you this or buy you that or get you into that orchestra." We both felt it would be much healthier if I did it on my own. The *Young Concert Artists* was absolutely crucial — it was the turning point. I am not quite sure what I would have been able to do without them.

P.E. What did you play at your debut?

ZUKERMAN The Fauré *Fantasy*, the Poulenc *Sonata*, the Mozart *Andante* and I played the Beethoven *Serenade* with Pinky and Michael Tree. Michael Tree is the violist with the Guarneri Quartet and his son was born that night at six o'clock and yet he came. It was very lovely of him. It was a very special night with Pinky and him as guests artists.

P.E. How do you organize your life today?

ZUKERMAN I always think of my life as being something like a Chinese menu. Sometimes I travel with Pinky, sometimes alone, sometimes I stay at home with the girls, sometimes we all go.

P.E. What are various typical days for you?

ZUKERMAN I can give you various "typicals" — I feel very Darwinian about our life. It's adapt or die. Survival of the fittest. I mean, if I am going to go to London and wish I was in New York, I would be in trouble. I have to get to London and try to adapt as fast as I can. We do that because if you are a musician and you have been travelling — you are a gypsy at heart. Wherever you are and you make music — it's the same. It's the surroundings that change. I try to keep a schedule and I have discovered, since my oldest daughter is four and a half and the baby is two, I find that if I can do what I do *away* from them — they're happier. I finally got a studio around the corner from here. It's just one room but it just makes all the difference in the world. Babies do not understand closed door policy. If I am practicing in a closed room, it's very hard for a baby who wants her mommy to accept that. She feels shut out. But if I leave and I leave them with someone they love, then there is generally no problem. My typical day is that I get up at six-thirty or seven with the children. I am a very light sleeper. I have never been able to hear them and not get up. So I get up and have breakfast with them. The older one goes to school so I take her to the school bus at eight thirty. And at that time, I will either play with the baby a little bit or go to my studio usually at nine or nine-thirty and stay there until lunchtime. I was worried when I got this space of my own.

P.E. "A Room of One's Own" — Virginia Woolf . . . why were you worried?

ZUKERMAN That I wouldn't use it. That I would get there and feel like a pampered princess. But I find that I covet it and when I get there — first of all, it's a sixth floor walk up, so by the time I get there, I am not about to run out for candy. I'm really there. I practice hard and I work on the things that are up and coming. Then I usually have lunch with the children and if I don't have a rehearsal or a meeting, I'll do something with the children — take them to the park and there are a lot of things to be done in the house and I do the cooking. There is generally a concert to go to at night or a play. We have a busy social life. I am involved in many different music making projects. I play recitals with Pinky, I do my solo things, I am playing with a guitarist named Carlos Bonnel — we've recorded for Columbia. There is a lot of interesting repertoire for flute and guitar like Giuliani and Diabelli and very nice little different gems. Then I have a trio with Jerome Lowenthal, pianist and Jeffrey Solow, cellist. There is also some very beautiful music for piano, flute and cello. We also get to play sonatas. I am also just beginning to work with a singer named Robert White, a tenor. We are doing some luscious things not for this season but the season after. Life is very, very full.

P.E. Are you and your husband still visiting Israel every year? Do you try to arrange your schedules so you can travel together as much as possible?

ZUKERMAN We haven't really been there in two years. Pinky's father died last year so he was back. We try to be together as much as we can. When we are both going to be in Europe, we try to do our work at the same time. I've got a few things in London and a recording so we've taken a flat and we have the girls with us — until they are so seriously involved in school, we will be able to take them for long stretches of time. We are planning to go less and less to Europe because of the children. We want them to have a feeling of home. The children come first. Absolutely.

P.E. Even for Pinky?

ZUKERMAN Especially for Pinky. When I had the children he cancelled everything just so he could be present at their birth. He is the most solicitous and wonderful father. His naturalness comes over in the way he handles them. He is just this great big bear for them.

P.E. Before having the children, how did you balance your life?

ZUKERMAN I found it difficult actually. I travelled with Pinky everywhere and that was very difficult in terms of losing my sense of identity. I was very much involved in what he was doing. I found it very difficult to hold on to things . . . to what *I* could do.

P.E. Did this situation gradually dawn on you? What did you do about it?

ZUKERMAN It gradually dawned on me. I began realizing that I was feeling wonderful when Pinky played a concert yet it was *he* who was playing the concert. It began to feel silly when people would say congratulations to me. But the excitement of being in Europe has never worn off. I was very much inundated with sensory responses to things. I was very happy to be travelling but I began to sense . . . being at sea. Travelling with him all the time, I had to do a lot of adapting.

P.E. Who had to do the most adapting?

ZUKERMAN Me. But it depends on the situation. I happen to be married to someone who is a great artist, who has a great mind and who has a mission, which is simply to play. There is no way that could ever change or would I ever want it to change. When we were married he was eighteen and we didn't know things would happen as fast as they did. We weren't given time to adjust to it properly — it just happened — "bang" and there we were — in Paris, London, Vienna, Munich, Amsterdam — one day after the next. His adapting wasn't done in the same way that mine was because he was playing. I find that if I am schlepping around to Godforsaken places and I am playing — I feel fine. But if I'm schlepping behind some-

one and carrying his suitcase, it's very hard. I did have a good time. I visited the museums, listened to rehearsals and learned a lot that way. I read a lot and met people — I walked around and I was fascinated but I had an urge in myself towards self-expression. If I didn't have that it probably would be a perfect existence for me. But somehow having the children: The children are the focus of our lives. We are very lucky to have beautiful, wonderful, bright and healthy children. I don't travel as much anymore. I simply can't. At first we took them around with us. We took Arianna — by the time she was ten months old she'd been to Europe four times. Then we went through the war in Israel in 1973 and she was ten months old — that changed a great deal for me.

P.E. In what way did the war change you?

ZUKERMAN I'm reticent to talk about it because it makes it all sound like clichés but you go back to certain basic truths. You realize what certain things mean to you. During that war I found out what music means to me. We were there when the war broke out and to me war is something that happens on television — not the real thing — but there I was with a crying baby and three seconds away from Damascus. There was a blackout and I was horrified. Pinky was to give a concert and I said, "How could you make music with boys dying, shooting each other, blowing each other up thirty miles from here?" They decided to go ahead with the concert. I went to the concert and there was a blackout — absolutely pitch black. There were air raids every two seconds. And when I heard music for the first time — even through the air raid sirens, it seemed to me to express what art, culture and everything we strive for really is, to say something about man, mankind and about humanity together. Music has the power to go beyond our mundane life. It is as simple as that. I had always known this but I *experienced* it. Hearing Beethoven that night was a very moving experience for me and I stopped being nervous. Life becomes very precious when it's threatened.

P.E. Do you want to pursue a solo career?

ZUKERMAN I am very actively pursuing a solo career. I will never be playing a hundred and twenty concerts a year, in any event, and I will always be able to arrange things so that I will go for one or two days and come back. My children are used to separations. I see it as healthy. I don't see it as necessary to be here all the time. If it was the sort of life where I had to be on the road for four or five weeks at a time — then I would find it difficult. But I feel that right now I am at my strongest point. I can see that I am physically in good shape and that I can handle it. Travelling is a very tiring existence, but I don't see it ending. I feel that the pieces are falling together and that now I am able to make music on a level that I am pleased with. I feel that there is tremendous need for improvement but I see now *what* to do. I have more of a sense of what direction to move into when I look at a piece.

P.E. What has helped you to sense your musical direction?

ZUKERMAN Understanding music more, listening to it more and playing. I gave one or two concerts in

Aspen last summer in July. I didn't play my first concert again until October of last fall — so there were two or three months during which I didn't perform at all. Then I had to get on the stage in Hamburg, Germany, which is a major capital of the world, and play. It felt like alien territory. I felt that it went well, but it was alien territory. Then after a few concerts I began to feel comfortable. What has made me feel more comfortable has been in the doing of it. The more concerts you play the better you play. I feel very fortunate to have a full and rich life. Children are absolutely essential to my perspective.

P.E. What pieces do you consider the most challenging for the flute that you would like to play.

ZUKERMAN There are several projects that I would like to do. I would like to perform all six or seven Bach Sonatas at once. I would like to learn some more modern works for example Boulez's *Sonatine*. I haven't yet learned Berio's *Sequenza*. I want to play the work of George Crumb. I would like to learn some new techniques on the flute like circular breathing, singing while playing. One of the things that I regret very much and I would stress to young players is not being able to memorize music.

P.E. Did you play anything from memory at the audition for Young Concert Artists?

ZUKERMAN Some things I did but I have discovered that with the children and with Pinky — I'm constantly prefacing everything with a list of my husband, my children, my house, my travelling! Because of all of the above, I find that I cannot play without the music. I am too distracted. I just can't do the kind of digging in that you need for the memorizing. If I had done it as a kid now it would be a lot easier. But now for me to memorize and play comfortably, I would have to work hours and hours and I don't have hours and hours.

P.E. What is most exciting for you right now?

ZUKERMAN Seeing my children when they come home with Pinky on Sunday. Most exciting things are prospects always. It's the future always; and enjoying the present. I think you have to live ninety percent in the present. I find most exciting for me are the things I want to do. I think that if you ever get to a stage in your musical life when there are not many projects ahead and that there aren't things to be done and that it's all repetition — then you are in big trouble. I feel excited that I am still enthusiastic. My enthusiasm has grown and I really want to play. You have to do enough performing to know if you really like it. As a child when I had to get up in front of P.T.A. assemblies, I would get nervous and get stomach aches. I wasn't the natural extrovert that you need to be — to be a real performer. I think that I have been able to develop certain aspects of my personality. When I am feeling well and when I am feeling in shape, I truly enjoy going out and playing.

P.E. So you have discovered that you like to play the flute.

ZUKERMAN Yes! I was up in Halifax, Nova Scotia and I bumped into a girl who came to the concert and I had known her fourteen years ago. She's playing first flute up in Halifax and she said, "Here we are fourteen years after we have been in Aspen together and we're still crazy about the flute. Isn't that something?"

P.E. How long have you been playing the flute?

ZUKERMAN Since I was ten and now I am thirty-two. It's twenty-two years that I've been playing. I dabbled at it as a kid, now I'm devoted to it. One of the wonderful things about music is its endless interest — there is always more and more to find in it. I feel like I'm just at the start of a long and beautiful voyage. Playing is a tremendous outlet. It's one of the reasons why performers who perform a lot are tremendously healthy. They don't put much emphasis on how each performance is but on the performance itself. You actually have the experience. A performer has this lucky built in thing. He just gets up there and here it is.

BERNARD GOLDBERG

BERNARD GOLDBERG

Born in Illinois, Bernard Goldberg studied with Kiburz and Torno and at the age of sixteen made his debut with the St. Louis Symphony. He studied at the Juilliard School of Music as a scholarship pupil of Georges Barrere, with Lucien Lavaillotte in Paris, and with Marcel Moyse at the Marlboro Music Festival. He spent two years of special study in Bach interpretation with Diran Alexanian and private coaching with Pablo Casals.

Mr. Goldberg joined the Cleveland Orchestra and became principal flutist at the age of 21. Since 1947 Mr. Goldberg has been principal flutist with the Pittsburgh Symphony, appearing frequently as soloist. He has performed as soloist in the Prades Music Festivals under the direction of Pablo Casals and in the Casals Festivals in San Juan, Puerto Rico. He has been principal flutist in the Mozart Festival Orchestra at the Lincoln Center for the Performing Arts in New York City, appearing as soloist in all the flute concertos by Mozart.

Mr. Goldberg teaches at the Duquesne University School of Music where he conducts the University Orchestra and Opera Workshop. He is associate conductor of the Pittsburgh Youth Symphony, a member of the Music Viva Trio, and is associated with the University of Pittsburgh. During the summer Mr. Goldberg teaches at the Temple University Institute. He was a founding member of the Board of the National Flute Association and its president in 1974–75. Mr. Goldberg also edits flute material and records "master class" cassettes for Edu-Tainment Publishing Company.

SETTING

"Music is the highest manifestation of the human spirit." Smiling, Bernard Goldberg's expressive hands embraced the air and his kind, brown eyes widened.

He is a discontented man but a self-fulfilling one. Among his dissatisfactions are the state of the world, wars, the quality of music and music education and the poverty of spirit and vision.

Throughout the one and a half hour interview, Mr. Goldberg was relaxed and spoke with ease and an intense concern for his students and music educators to realize that "music has content."

Dressed in a blue blazer, white shirt and grey trousers, as he had breakfast in the coffee shop of the Hotel Wellington in New York City, he looked discriminating and elegant. After breakfast, we proceeded with the interview in his hotel room where he sat by his desk and I in an armchair facing him. He spoke easily and with a warmth and grace sharpened by a keen wit. He was happy and nostalgic when recounting his youth, student days and his first attempts at playing the flute. When asked what he wished for his students, his brown eyes brightened and he said, "That they include in their playing the clarity of the sun, the color of growing things and the perfumes of nature."

His professional demeanor surfaced as his rehearsal time approached. He looked down to his watch, frowning, afraid of being late — "I've got to get ready for my rehearsal now."

INTERVIEW

P.E. You have studied with Kiburz, Torno, Georges Barrere, Lucien Lavaillotte in Paris, Marcel Moyse at the Marlboro Music Festival, Diran Alexanian and Pablo Casals. How did each of these teachers influence you?

GOLDBERG First, I'll start with Mr. Kiburz because it brings us to the problem a friend asked me about while I was practicing at his house — he's a clarinetist. He asked, "When you practice scales are you using vibrato?" I said, "I hope not." Flute players make such a great fuss about vibrato. He then asked, "When do you use vibrato?" I said, "When the music needs it." "How?," he asked. I said, "I just feel the intensity of the phrase and then something happens." "Oh," he said. Mr. Kiburz had me play a concert waltz from *La Traviata* and told me that the melody was sad and that I should feel sad. He demonstrated and there was vibrato in his tone. Then he said, "Now, you play with that kind of expression," and I did. What I want to point out is that music has content no matter what some very famous composers have said. It's more than a sound duration. Mr. Torno impressed this upon me. When I went to Barrere, he tried to teach me about taste and about the beauty of flute playing as a vehicle of expression of human feelings. I was in the Cleveland Orchestra for three years and while I was there I expected to study with Mr. Moyse in Paris but this was right after the Second World War, and although I had a passport, I couldn't get a visa from the French government. Instead, I spent a year in New York and through the influence of friends I was accepted by Diran Alexanian who was a cello teacher and a great teacher of chamber music and a specialist in the interpretation of the music of Johann Sebastian Bach. I went to him thinking it was just a matter of approaching the Bach sonatas. But he was a great pedagogue who taught me about the analysis of every note and, how to, as he put it, "Reach into the composer's process." Obviously nobody can be Johann Sebastian Bach, but we can try to figure out how he happened to put down the ink in the way that he did.

P.E. You cannot reach into his impulse but you can understand his musical reasons.

GOLDBERG Yes, purely the musical reasons and the inter-reaction. The relationships of the counterpoint and everything that has to do with the craft of composition. Without that, we haven't begun except in a dilettante way to comprehend what we are supposed to convey to our listeners. For some people, this is instinctive but for others it has to be thought through.

P.E. Deciding on an attitude by defining the emotion you should have?

GOLDBERG Defining the kind of reaction one should have to certain musical events within the composition. For example, the harmonic palette of the Baroque composer is fairly restrained in comparison to the palette of the nineteenth century composer. A cadence in a composition by Bach or Handel is a great event whereas in Wagner you wouldn't pay any attention to it. One has to react. In order to teach me, a single line player — since my keyboard playing had always been limited, and, of course, with many keyboard players, it's just in the fingers and not in the head, Mr. Alexanian devised a pedagogy method which was part of experiments that he and Paul Hindemith were doing. He made me do graphs of the Bach Chorales — of the harmonic progressions and the degree of tension that the progressions should create in the performer or listener as they become more distant from the tonic and how they move in relation to the element of time and to forging things ahead. For months, I didn't play a note for Mr. Alexanian. All we did was analyze chorales but eventually we got around to working on sonatas. He made me write out each part and the score — not just the keyboard part but four staves with their correct voice leading at all times. You will find, in some editions of the Bach Flute Sonatas, realizations that might be convenient for a pianist but if three singers were to sing those lines over the bass, they would find that they would eventually sound like they were singing *Pierre Lunaire* because the lead voice is so poor. One of the main things that I learned from Mr. Alexanian, was the habit of questioning anything that I saw in front of me and to take the time to sit down and with the proper background and information, to try to find my own answers to the musical problems which I might encounter in an interpretation or performance of any given piece. That is why just imitating a teacher is not enough. A teacher must teach the students, the prospective artists, to think for himself. You can't always wait for the teacher to say, "Take a breath here."

P.E. When did you study with Marcel Moyse?

GOLDBERG I had been corresponding with Mr. Moyse since I was in high school. There is the Mozart Flute and Harp Concerto and I bought his recording of it. I would spend hour after hour trying to imitate this mythological figure who was an important influence in my life. Anyway, I was recommended to Moyse by one of his earliest pupils, Lucien Lavaillotte, who was the principal flutist of the Paris Opera and an excellent teacher for me.

P.E. You studied with Lavaillotte in Paris?

GOLDBERG Yes. My father's family is originally from Warsaw, Poland and some of them, in their western migration, didn't get any farther than Paris. I have cousins in Paris and we have become very close. Mr. Lavaillotte, who was the son of a coal miner, a really poor kid, had gotten into the Paris Conservatory and was eventually unhappy with the teacher there and began to sneak out to Marcel Moyse, who was pretty young then too, for a lesson. He was a great admirer of Moyse but I don't think the admiration was returned because of events that took place during the war.

P.E. I believe Moyse left Paris during the war because he refused to teach at the Paris Conservatory during the German Occupation.

GOLDBERG Yes ... I don't know all the details. They both tell different stories. I saw a documentary about how sordid the people turned out to be amongst themselves during the German Occupation. Anyway, with Moyse I began working for clarity, refinement and purity of attack. The precision of articulation. I studied with him privately during the summer and most of my free time was spent with my cousins. I regret I didn't have time to become involved with the Paris musical scene. I went to the Paris Opera as an outsider. I was not a very pushy person and I was the same as a student here in New York. Anyway, in 1950, I read in the *New York Times* that there was going to be a celebration of the death of Johann Sebastian Bach to be held in a little village in France. It was to be led by Pablo Casals. Alexanian and Casals were very closely associated. During the days of Casals, teaching in Paris, Alexanian would sometimes teach his class. At this point, I felt prepared because I had finished my second year as principal flutist in the Pittsburgh Symphony so I asked to be a part of the Casals Festival and I was accepted. In fact, I had met Alexander Schneider in Mr. Alexanian's apartment and Schneider was also studying Bach and chamber music with Alexanian. The Casals Festival was one of the greatest experiences of my musical and personal life.

P.E. How were you influenced by Casals?

GOLDBERG All of us in the orchestra were overwhelmed by the beauty of this old fellow and by his enormous love for the music and his ability to transcend all rules and systems of interpretation. There are many books written about rules and system and on Bach interpretation — we have to know the facts but there still has to be temperment. With Casals, it was like the music had just been written. The recordings he made in 1950 of the Brandenburg concertos are inferior technically to later recordings but muscially they are superior because they are more explicit in some of the statements he was striving towards. Casals said, "Bach is a volcano. Every note in Bach has to have juice." Bach was everything but a Herr Professor — the dedicated scholar. You have to have musical scholarship but as Alexanian said, "Without talent, there is nothing I could do." To see Casals bend over the music stand, weeping because of the beauty of the music and the experience — to see him work hard all morning and then rush home for a bite and then start practicing, was an inspiration. He was always this way until his very last years in Puerto Rico when he became ill. But the humanity of the man and his understanding of the musical content of Bach and Mozart — I said to him one day in Puerto Rico as we rehearsed the *Third Brahms Symphony*, "Oh, Met, you do that so wonderfully. It must have been the way Brahms wanted it done — the way he composed it." Casals was a composer as well, so in studying a score he could re-think the composer's process. He said to me, "It's always been the greatest regret of my life that I never met Brahms. Did you know that my career had already started when he was still alive? But it just never happened." To have been in contact with this man whose career had started in the nineteenth century during the Romantic period and to have learned from him this humanistic and optimistic point of view about music and the human race, has been an extraordinary influence on my life.

P.E. I read where a student of Casals played a piece for him badly, except for one passage which he played su-

perbly, and he asked Casals what he thought of it and Casals said he had played it well but the student said, "I played it terribly." Casals replied, "No, you did one thing perfectly. Only bad people remember and live for bad things."

GOLDBERG He was always very kindly and always tried to find good things and then it was up to the student to perceive what had to be done in order for the rest of it to be good.

P.E. Since you are a flutist, how did Casals, a cellist, help you technically?

GOLDBERG For example, before a performance of *St. Mathew's Passion,* I went to Casals and asked him to help me with the obbligato "Alas, now my Saviour is gone." He showed me various things to do and explained the reasons for the musical drama and helped me with intonation. He didn't have much to say about what I was doing technically, although when he was a little boy, he said he had played the flute in the symphony orchestra. He said, "Aren't you glad I didn't continue? You would have had some competition." Another time, I went to him with the Mozart Harp and Flute concerto and I played it through and Casals began discussing Beethoven's *Fourth Symphony* and eventually we talked about Beethoven's *Seventh Symphony* and about three hours later, we got back to the Mozart Flute and Harp concerto. He wanted to fill me in musically on the kind of background or sense of music making which would give more life and meaning to the Mozart concerto itself.

P.E. I read he didn't like to play long notes — he liked to shorten them.

GOLDBERG He said variety is the law of nature and every note has its own personality and every phrase its own face and the face changes. I remember him saying that when the musical line rises there is a natural rise of dynamics and when it falls that there is a natural tendency for the dynamic level to fall. Otherwise, I do believe he required a penetration of what the composer had written and then tried to make what the musician found there audible to the listener. It's not enough to say, "It's this way." You have to sit still and practice until you could convey what you find under the ink and paper.

P.E. When was the first time you heard the flute?

GOLDBERG I wanted to play the flute since I was eight or nine years old. My brother, Norman, played clarinet. I thought he was the most marvelous person in the world and I still do. I wanted to play duets and he thought the flute would be nice. I remember going to hear a band concert in a church in which my brother was playing and it must have been just terrible because after I had been playing the flute six months, I was accepted into the band.

P.E. Had you had any formal lessons yet?

GOLDBERG I began when I was in sixth grade but nowadays that would be considered late. Now kiddos come to me and they have been playing flute since third grade — of course, they haven't learned anything. The whole class gets flutes. My first teacher was the junior high school band director who was about as qualified to teach flute as I am to swim the English Channel. But, luckily, the conservatory from St. Louis established a branch in Belleville—but it really was an outlet for the accordian. The accordian sales were beginning to boom at the time. The conservatory in St. Louis had in the past very excellent teachers and one of them was John F. Kiburz who had been the principal flutist of the St. Louis Symphony for twenty-seven years. When he heard Georges Barrere, he realized that this was the way he wanted to play the flute so he quit his job and left his wife and came to New York to study with Barrere and was eventually playing second flute in the Damrosch Orchestra. Then his wife wired that the St. Louis Symphony wanted him back as the principal flutist so he returned to St. Louis and some years later came over to Belleville once a week to teach. I was very lucky that at tha age of eleven I had a very good teacher although I didn't practice much. I could have done a lot better if I had paid attention to my parents and practiced.

P.E. You were stubborn?

GOLDBERG I was a very stubborn child. I didn't practice because they said I should practice.

P.E. What do you tell your students now about practicing?

GOLDBERG That if they don't practice, I can't be bothered with them. In any case, Mr. Kiburz must have been a very good man because in six months of studying with him, I was already winning contests at the seventh or eighth grade level. I was about twelve.

P.E. Your parents seemed encouraging and interested in your music.

GOLDBERG They encouraged me very much. My father, at that time, had a business of buying up old machinery from the coal mines. Southern Illinois is coal mining country. He would sell the used machine parts to the small family type coal mines. He was a salvage parts dealer. Belleville was mostly settled by Germans so there was an amazing amount of musical culture from the late nineteenth century in Germany. My older brother played the violin in the local amateur orchestra which is the second oldest amateur orchestra in America. It's called the Belleville Philharmonia which is an outgrowth of the Belleville Sinfonia which was obviously founded by the Germans.

P.E. How did this Germanic culture influence your music?

GOLDBERG Because of the fact that there was the opportunity for me, when I was fourteen years old, to play in an orchestra other than with the few scratchy violins in the school orchestra and to be able to play real literature. My heavens, when I think back to the first rehearsal and how many strings and violins there were—I was overwhelmed by the beauty of it all. I was finding the world I wanted to live in. When I was fifteen or so in St. Louis, I knew a fellow who had ambitions to be a french horn player and he founded a youth symphony. They asked Mr. Kiburz for a flutist and he suggested I go over. That was a new experience because they were young and good musicians playing in the orchestra in order to gain experience.

P.E. When did you take the flute seriously?

GOLDBERG When I was a sophomore in high school, the principal second violinist asked Mr. Kiburz, if he had a good student to learn the Mozart flute and harp concerto with his son Eddy Gesinski and Mr. Kiburz brought me the music. I eventually met the whole Gesinski family and became a sort of member of their family. Mrs. Gesinski was the harpist in the summer operetta and played piano and they convinced my parents that I had the potential to become a professional flutist.

P.E. What did your parents think about your musical career?

GOLDBERG They thought it was a wonderful idea but in later years when they discovered that there are limitations on the income and drawbacks in the work schedule of a symphony flutist, they were less enthusiastic and when my career was going to be centered in Pittsburgh, which, after all, is six hundred miles from St. Louis, they were not happy. But my father went down to the symphony office in Pittsburgh to negotiate and found out that I could do better financially so he said, "You know, Bernard, we would love to have you at home but your life is all ahead of you and ours is mostly beh it's my advice that you stay there and grow with that orchestra—it seems to have more possibilities than what is here now." The Gesinski's were wonderful to me. They helped me a great deal with details—the kind a student can't get in a weekly lesson.

P.E. What kind of details did they help you with?

GOLDBERG Mr. Gesinski was such a cracker about intonation. I remember, one fine day, I went to their home and he opened the door and said, "Your C is too sharp." He didn't say, "Hi, Bernie." It had been on his mind the whole week. He helped me with intensity and articulation.

P.E. When did you decide to come to New York and study with Georges Barrère?

GOLDBERG Even though I was studying with Torno, who was the principal flutist of the St. Louis Symphony, I had in mind, after I finished high school, to go to New York and study with Barrère. I was accepted at Juilliard and by Mr. Barrère.

P.E. How long did you study with Mr. Barrère?

GOLDBERG Three years.

P.E. Was it before or after his stroke?

GOLDBERG He had the stroke after I had been studying with him for one year. He was in his sixties but he seemed much older because he had burned the candle at all five ends. He was not well, although he certainly was a beautiful human being and a wonderful teacher. During my first year at Juilliard, he was still playing and there were times when he would demonstrate the vibrato—which was simply unforgettable because of the quality of his tone and the intensity of his communicative power. The things he would do in articulation were not only beautiful and clear but they were simply charming and winsome. After his stroke, when he came back to teaching, I was one of the first pupils he took back. I worked with him for the next two years and during the summer I would continue my studies with Mr. Torno in St. Louis.

P.E. Did you do any playing outside of your studies at Juilliard?

GOLDBERG Outside of Juilliard, I played in an Italian Opera Company which still exists here in New York on 89th and Broadway. I was so ignorant at that time that I thought that playing *Rigoletto* and *La Traviatta* was just terrible and so I used to bring Brahms songs and Bach Chorales to read during intermission. We were paid six dollars for a rehearsal and a performance—at the time, probably union scale was ten dollars. The singers were unbelievably bad and the conductor was just learning his craft. It was good for us as young musicians to learn this music because they teach one to sing. It is through singing that one learns to sing throurgument.

P.E. Do you work out difficult passages by singing?

GOLDBERG Surely and Casals said to memorize as quickly as possible so that you could get to the music behind the ink and paper and then in the car or whatever to sing and see what happens.

P.E. Who was the best musical influence in your life?

GOLDBERG I discovered that the one best musical influence in my life was my mother's singing. She had no musical or vocal training but evidently at one time before the outbreak of the flu in 1918, she had had a lovely quality. She is an extremely musical person. Just listening to me practice, she eventually learned a little of this concerto and a little of that sonata. She is constantly singing. I learned to listen very carefully to what she was doing because so much of it was right musically.

P.E. You have studied other instruments?

GOLDBERG I should have been at the piano when I was four years old because I believe that anyone who wants to be anybody at all—a doctor, an engineer or a lawyer should play a little piano. We are not all going to be Shakespearian actors but we can certainly read. Without reading, you cannot get into the literature. Without the ability to read music at a keyboard instrument of some sort, it gets to be awfully difficult to get into the music—other than in single lines. As part of general culture, everyone should have a little keyboard training and at least some solfege so that looking at those symbols on the page convey information — just as symbols on the paper convey information — that's part of our heritage. I really believe that people are not only robbed of the ability to enjoy this heritage but by denying the youngster that kind of an education, it will fragment kids because the arts are very basic to human existence.

P.E. How do you think our society treats the arts?

GOLDBERG The arts are split off therefore our personality and individuality is collectively and personally unwhole. Primitive man's artistic expression was part of the practical.

P.E. What do you stress most in your teaching about breathing?

GOLDBERG Barrère said that you should not breathe when you need to but when the music needs to. Also, it is a matter of finding what the composer has written. I see editions of etudes and even of compositions in which the so called editor seems to have a stencil. He puts a breath in exactly the same place no matter what the form or structure might be or what the construction of the musical line is and no matter what the harmonic progressions are. This is an example of ignorant musical thinking. I cannot separate taking a breath from re-creating a phrase. The composer created it and it is up to us to re-create it. What the composer did in space on paper, we have to do in time. The basic dimension of music is time. We can make music with a knock, an object—the variety is infinite. We have to re-create the phrase in time and the dimension of time always comes of its structure and of its origin. As for the mechanics of breathing, I tell my students to breathe as singers do. The breathing problems are essentially those of a singer. There are some beautiful pictures of Barrére which are straight forward and open because he was always emphasizing, "Play straight forward and frankly."

P.E. How do you teach a student to study a piece of literature?

GOLDBERG I begin with the music. That may sound goofy, but a lot of people begin with the recording. I might listen to a recording or a student might listen to a recording but only to find out if it's an interesting piece, but not as a means of study. The first thing one has to do is to analyze the music. To find out the difficulties and analyze the difficulties — narrowing them down to, let's say, a combination of three or four notes that might be of difficulty to the fingers or a combination of fingers and lips and working on those and gradually fitting them in, but to play the whole piece from beginning to end, over and over again, and never mastering the particular small combination that creates the problems, is a waste of time.

P.E. Do you think of any special images to loosen up a tight throat?

GOLDBERG Just the other day, I was thinking about what Mr. Wummer said, "Blow warm air." Think that the air, which is coming out, is very warm and that you are steaming up the window or about to clean your eye glasses.

P.E. Do you teach vibrato?

GOLDBERG I don't—except by imitation. Mr. Moyse says he feels hot in his chest, his throat and trunk. I say to some of my flute students that they have a high throat—that the throat is high instead of opened all the way down to the bottom of the lungs.

P.E. Do you talk about the projection of sound?

GOLDBERG No, I don't talk about sound projection, but I do say that I want the sound out in front of the flute. I have been lucky to have played obbligatos for singers and at their lessons I would see the teachers work with the singers on the vocal line. When Mr. Barrére said, "Play frankly and straight forward," then I could think of projecting the tone out through the mask. A flute player should never permit his face to feel frozen or stiff — contrary to some teachers who say that the mouth is supposed to be very tense. I just can't believe that they can produce a communicative sound that way. Projection is a matter of purity of tone and again referring back to the singer's technique, which is getting the most amount of tone with the least amount of air and not to waste air on the edges of the sound. There are flutists who talk about the grain and it just diffuses the sound. The sound has to be pure.

P.E. Can you tell me how you make a pure sound?

GOLDBERG First of all, you must have the concept. The lips must not be more tense than is necessary. The mouth must not be opened more than is necessary. I do not mean to clench the jaw or pinch the lips but just to do the minimum which will produce the maximum results and to conceive of the air stream as always flowing across the wet parts of the lip. The air stream should never be in contact with the dry outside part of the lip. A flutist does not permit the corners of his lips to be down because then the dry part of the upper lip will be in contact with the air stream and the throat gets dry. Now, about the matter of cutting through the orchestra, I think of it as singing through the orchestra. There is a very famous Wagnerian singer whose voice cuts through the orchestra but she is, for my taste, the Isolde that belongs in the movie Clockwork Orange. You should never hear any funny sounds outside of the voice. It's when people force that they don't focus. But the focus is, first of all, in your mind — it's the concept.

P.E. What helps you to focus? Certain images? The sun?

GOLDBERG Yes it's interesting that you should mention the sun because once in a lesson with Mr. Moyse in Marlboro — I was working on the first exercise in one of his books, he said to play the B to Bb like the sun, just pouring out over the whole world, and that the b and e flat must be like God's love. This may sound old fashioned to some people. Once, after my talk on Mr. Moyse's book Development and Interpretation, a flute teacher said, "I read your article and it's very romantic." I thought to myself, "Poor fellow, what does he think music is all about? Is he teaching all these youngsters just to play the flute?" A flute player came to study with me and she said that a teacher at her college said to her that if she wanted to become a flute player she would have to think of herself as a mechanic. What an ugly way to think. Is one going to dedicate one's life to that?

P.E. How close do you hold your fingers above the flute?

GOLDBERG One of the first things that Mr. Barrére worked on was movement of the fingers. As a general rule, he didn't let the fingers go more than a quarter or half an inch above the keys. I once played the Lizst E Flat Concerto for Mr. Barrére and I said, "This doesn't sound right," and he said, "Play it for me." Much to my surprise, he got up and stared at my hands. He saw that on the E-F-E I raised my little finger, of the left hand, too high, so the F got too pale and too sharp and the same for the A-B-A — the B had no color. To raise the fingers very far is a waste of time and it necessitates a very fast movement of the fingers, which is bound to result in a physical loss because of the distance.

P.E. Do you ever use alternate fingerings?

GOLDBERG There are occasions when I use alternate fingerings. But it has to be an extremely rapid passage and almost always in a tutti passage. I try to avoid alternate fingerings in any exposed passage because I look for the purist quality. People come to me and play Afternoon of a Faun with twenty fingerings for the C sharp. Of course, the C sharp is a difficult note, but that strange, open flute sound, which the C sharp can produce, is evidently the color that Debussy wanted and the intonation and quality he wanted. Barrère said that if Debussy wanted to write that passage for the english horn, he knew what the english horn sounded like. Barrére played the first performance of Afternoon of a Faun. Debussy was still adjusting the orchestration.

P.E. Playing the same pieces in the symphony season after season, how do you keep your playing fresh?

GOLDBERG There are some pieces, which after awhile, do become boring — even some new pieces, which are boring. But the great master works are never boring and they always present their problems. Years ago, when I was in the Cleveland Orchestra, I remember playing the second flute and Maurice Sharp was playing first. It was the Beethoven Seventh and he said, "You know, I think I'm making progress until we play this piece again." The problems are always a little bit more difficult than the development of one's playing.

P.E. And you only discover the level of the problems according to the level you are at.

GOLDBERG Exactly. Casals once said, "I have been working on this piece for fifty years and I don't have it yet — maybe I'll get it today." I gave a recital in Pittsburgh and I played the Schubert Variations and I know that I played them better now than I did twenty years ago, but it isn't any easier. Keeping fresh is just barely trying to keep up and at the same time one has to learn new music. I premiere many new pieces. Like Streams and Willows.

P.E. Robert Morris's piece — I talked to him about it and I saw the score — you had a lot of new techniques to learn in a short time.

GOLDBERG Yes, I had a lot to do in trying to learn at least enough avant garde techniques to play that piece.

P.E. How did you prepare yourself technically for Streams and Willows?

GOLDBERG Insufficiently. The manuscript was badly scored. I must confess I couldn't study it for very long because my eyes would get too tired. The orchestra parts were also bad — it's a wonder that it got performed at all.

P.E. I think he had to put the score together at the last moment because the call from Pittsburgh was a surprise. Since you say it was badly scored, why did you play it?

GOLDBERG It wasn't imposed on me. I found it interesting because I could see the compositional skills involved and I could imagine the sounds that would be produced.

P.E. Would you play it again?

GOLDBERG Surely. I would even play it with the score I have.

P.E. Did you practice differently for this piece than for a classical piece?

GOLDBERG First of all, there are multi-phonics involved and I had to learn the fingerings. I had to practice to get the embouchure necessary for that particular combination of sounds. I can't say that I was always successful, after all, I can't spend the time that a person specializing in avant garde music can. I tried. I have been invited to play *Song of the Whale* by George Crumb and at Marlboro, a few years ago, I played *Eleven Echoes of Autumn*. I think it's the only piece that has ever been booed at Marlboro. But I feel that it's necessary for me as a human being and as a musician to at least try and as a functioning member of the musical community to lend my skills, my knowledge and my prestige — to put it frankly, to do some new repertory, whether it's avant garde music, old music or nineteenth century music. If I do a new piece, it might attract more serious listeners, at least around Pittsburgh, than some student would. It's the responsibility of the mature, established artist, who has some kind of reputation and some kind of following to do some new pieces. I just can't believe certain famous pianists who stick to three of Beethoven's piano concertos and maybe three concertos of other composers and make a whole art of that. Maybe they practice other things at home, I don't know.

P.E. They take risks at home.

GOLDBERG But that's not any kind of artistic responsibility.

P.E. What skills are needed to play in the orchestra?

GOLDBERG Dependability. The ability to play all the notes at the right time. Cooperation — which includes the skill of playing in tune with oneself and one's colleagues and, of course, the ability to reflect in one's own playing the interpretative thoughts of the conductor which involves, after all, all the skills involved in music-making. In the orchestra, I cannot stop and discuss certain things and maybe say, "How about trying it this way?," as I could in a trio. The conductor is the boss who has the distinct responsibility of leadership. Some impose themselves as a dictator but we have always been fortunate because Steinberg always wanted us to contribute and was willing to make music with us under his leadership but not under his dictatorship.

P.E. What would you like your students to remember most after they leave you?

GOLDBERG That's my way of playing, and what I have tried to teach is an attempt to play the flute in the most efficient way possible and to play with freedom, with openness and verve, so the performer can communicate the infinite variety of expression which is contained in the enormous literature of music. But I don't insist upon certain ways of playing. As I said, the muscles of the lips, the support of the lips by the jaw, the open chest, the relaxed throat, the quiet, efficient use of the fingers, the use of the tongue — just enough — not more, unless the music calls for extraneous tongue sounds.

P.E. What do you expect of yourself now?

GOLDBERG That's a very complex question for me to answer. I would like to be able to pass on my own musical culture and efficiency. I would like to be able to concertize more outside of the orchestra. There has never been such a tremendous population growth of flute players. But whether there is a rise in the quality of musical interest, I don't know. If you look at the record catalogues, and see the number of recordings of the Mozart Flute Concertos — it's pretty comparable to recordings of the Mozart Violin Concerts. I think, that little by little, a rise in musical quality will happen. Organizations such as local flute clubs and the National Flute Association will be very helpful.

P.E. Do you have a wish for your students?

GOLDBERG I would wish them good health. To learn to study music, and to think more in terms of content — that knowing or re-thinking the composer's process, is only part of it. The composer's process is only the mechanics of the composition. It's not yet content. I would recommend that they study string quartets, the scores and performances and then a lot of practicing out in the country where they can breathe fresh air, but I don't mean among the sheep. To be able to experience nature, and, of course, I think it's a very great thing to practice projection out of doors and find a tree a hundred yards away and play for that particular spot on the tree, but never forcing, and to include in one's music-making the clarity of the sunshine and the color of growing things and the perfumes of nature. I think hours and years spent in this fragrant isolation can not help but raise the quality of inner experience. Once, in a class at Marlboro, some oboist played a piece for Mr. Moyse, and it really was not bad — it had some color, but there was no content, and for once, Moyse looked helpless. He is such an inventive and perceptive man, but he sat for a moment and he finally looked at the young musician and said, "Go look at the sunset." I would also wish that young musicians would study more of what they are playing, for example, when I learned and continued to study the Beethoven Symphonies, I didn't learn them from an orchestra setting, I learned them from the scores, so that I could see and study the function of the flute part as part of the whole. In 1964, Mr. Casals came to Pittsburgh and played the *Brandenburg Concertos* and taught some classes. During one of the rehearsals of the *Brandenburg*, he looked over at one of the violinists of the Pittsburgh Symphony who was notably sour, and who has been an old man since he was thirty, and he said to this fellow, "You ought to learn the other parts as well as your own. You will not only be a better musician but you will have a better life." Perhaps students, like all young people, are too limited in their outlook. And of course, it takes a long time in life, altogether, until one's individual activities begin to transcend the eye and that the eye becomes part of the larger activity.

P.E. What do you mean by the larger activity? Young people have more distractions today—many more choices to make. I think it's difficult.

GOLDBERG I suppose for a very good reason because they are not willing to feel part of the larger activity—the world. After all, there has been World War II and the holocaust and add to that the debacle of American politics and society—it is difficult to want to be a part of that and not allow the weeds to cover the vision of western civilization. I agree with Mr. Casals, music is not only a game of sound and time in duration, that at least for us musicians, music is the highest manifestation of the human spirit.

THOMAS NYFENGER

THOMAS NYFENGER

Thomas Daniel Nyfenger was born on October 6, 1936 in Cleveland, Ohio.

He graduated from the Cleveland Institute of Music where he studied with Maurice Sharp and received a Masters in music.

He has been on the faculties of the Cleveland Institute of Music, Sarah Lawrence College, Vassar College, Purchase State University of New York, Queens College, the summer faculty of Boudoin College, and was the co-ordinator for the wind department at the Yale School of Music where he is currently teaching.

He has played in the Indianapolis Symphony, with the Aeolian Chamber Players, in residence with the Contemporary Chamber Ensemble at Rutgers State University, the New York City Ballet Orchestra for five seasons, the Mostly Mozart Festival for three seasons, the New York Woodwind Quintet, the Midnight Bach Concerts, and with Arthur Weisberg. He also enjoys giving master classes.

Mr. Nyfenger has recorded with various ensembles for Columbia, Decca and C.R.I.

He has two children, Paula and Julie-Ann. Mr. Nyfenger enjoys sports and weight lifting.

SETTING

Mr. Nyfenger was stirring a pot of chicken soup in his rented beach house in East Haven, Connecticut. Sunday soup was on and he greeted me with a firm handshake. "I rented the house for a year. It's furnished and has eight rooms," he said showing me into the living room where a bean bag, made by a friend, faced the television set and in front of the stone fireplace was a weight lifting bar, which he invited me, with a smile to lift. "Instead of jogging in the cold, I'm lifting weights."

In a back sunny room, which opened to the beach, was a stereo set and Paula Robison's record *The Romantic Flute*. "My favorite," he said and we returned to the dining room where we sat down at a long wooden table with music books and his flute at one end.

Mr. Nyfenger saved his soup for later.

Facing me, with his arm resting on the table, he was relaxed — a contrast to the bustle of meeting him on two previous occasions during lunch breaks from teaching at the Yale School of Music. He is handsome, with abundant black, curly hair, pale complexion and large dark eyes which are direct and miss nothing.

Throughout our conversation, his voice was steady and clear yet I sensed a vulnerability, a lunar yet dark essence which illuminates his world. He is a perfectionist. Intense, searching out extremes and risking to discover. He deals hard but honestly. And whether talking quietly or enthusiastically about playing or living, the core of integrity and purity centers him and the prism of his huge talent remains unswerving.

INTERVIEW

P.E. How did you develop your tone?

NYFENGER I listened to a lot of people, listened to a lot of records. I spent a couple of hours after midnight, when everything else was done, but this is about twenty years ago. I'd go up to the attic, put on the record player and try to figure out how the sound I was listening to was produced — how the player learned that particular sound since you can't actually study with everyone.

P.E. Who were the players that you listened to?

NYFENGER William Kincaid, Rampal, Julius Baker, Albert Tipton — just about everyone who had recordings out.

P.E. How old were you when you began this self-apprenticeship?

NYFENGER Sixteen.

P.E. Did you play another instrument before learning the flute?

NYFENGER Yes. I was a pianist. I played by ear from when I could reach the keys and studied from age nine to fourteen.

P.E. Why did you choose the play the flute?

NYFENGER I was trying to vibrate on the piano . . . then I started playing a little flute on my own — doing everything wrong. Then I began studying with Maurice Sharp. But since orchestral instruments have such a variety of tonal possibilities, the best thing for me to do was to imitate every style that was around and see what I could use. You know, I find that people don't want to spend any time at all experimenting. They want something that comes out right away and when they finish up their undergraduate studes, they feel they know everything there is to know. You try to talk people into doing anything else — anything different, any other quality, any other style and they're not interested.

P.E. What are they interested in?

NYFENGER They're interested in going somewhere, playing and getting all the right notes for the orchestra and the conductor and just becoming museum pieces — playing the same way for forty years! That is a shame. I just feel that when I've run out of things to try, as far as the possibilities of the instrument, then I might as well quit because it won't interest me anymore. There is only growth or death. Stagnation is death.

P.E. What were some important points that your teachers emphasized in your early study of the flute?

NYFENGER I never got too much advice about embouchure . . . I went to one fellow who said you should play a little lower on your lip and I did that for a while and experimented with it. Then someone else said, "Why don't you make your cheeks looser?," so, I did that for a few weeks to see what would happen . . . I did a lot of long tones and mirror looking. I'd say, "I like the way he did that piece," and I'd try to do it that way until I felt it was pretty close. I'd notice that my upper lip was

out a bit and it was making this certain tone — so, I'd work in that direction — do some careful long tones, some slow pieces. Moyse is very influential with his etude and tone building books. You can use them and you don't have to sound like him although he is a marvelous player. You can use these etudes and progressions, gradually increasing the size of the intervals . . . things like that.

P.E. Why is playing long tones so crucial to developing tone?

NYFENGER Well, if you play a straight-ahead long tone, be dissatisfied because what you do first you can always do better. While holding the note, manipulate the embouchure and the air and always try to improve. The problem is to carry a certain quality of tone — sonority — from one note down to other octaves without losing it. Maria Callas was often put down by people who said she sounded like she had three different voices — but a lot of people liked the different quality of the registers. You'll find, if you want to play a baroque piece which takes up two and a half octaves, you like to be able to make it sound homogeneous throughout. Not tubby and fat at the bottom, and light and brittle on top, so, you have to try to stretch and do the long tones like Moyse. As he once said, "Now, little by little we find the way to the low register." In other words, one note at a time, listening to each note as it goes down, so that it doesn't change too much until you find your way to the bottom.

P.E. It takes a lot of control . . . a lot of patience.

NYFENGER Patience, yes. But the problem is that people try to do that along with all their finger work, all their etudes and work at the sound at the same time — that is very difficult. I learned early, that when I started to fall behind a little bit I had to set aside some time when I wasn't going to worry about the tone so that I could develop the coordination. If you're worried only about whether you have the biggest tone or whether you play your etudes — you're never going to get anything done. So, go to work on the tone, then the fingers, and then put it all together.

P.E. How do you use your different moods to your advantage in your work?

NYFENGER When I feel very calm and a little bit overly patient — sort of dull, I can work carefully on fingering things, scales, arpeggios and etudes, because I don't find that I need a great imagination for it. Sometimes, with too much imagination you don't feel like working slowly, carefully on technique. You have to feel very much in a calm mood to take the time and work slowly . . . watch your fingers — that they're not moving too fast or too far or speeding up. But when you feel like experimenting, it's a good time to be working on tone. In other words, if you have to make preliminary sketches in art, you can do them in whatever mood you are in and draw the squares and plan out where things are going to go, but when you want to put in colors and the life into it, then you need to be in a different mood. Some people waste a lot of time saying that they don't feel like practicing when actually what they don't feel like doing is playing something beautiful at that time. So they should use the time when they don't feel like practicing to work on their technique. There's an anecdote about Alice Chalifoux of the Cleveland Orchestra who had a masters degree student, who had already played professionally—he was temperamental—the Sarah Bernhardt of the harp. One day he came in and said, "Oh, Mrs. Chalifoux, I don't feel like playing my lesson today." So she said to him, "Well, who in the hell asked you?" There are times when you don't feel that good but you do it. You play! I say, "Let's start doing it now and be realistic even though this is just a class—you are going to be a professional. I can feel terrible—have a head cold which makes it hard to hear and I could go in front of the mirror for a half hour and see if my fingers are moving right—I don't even have to blow."

P.E. Do you talk to your students about how to deal with competition?

NYFENGER The first thing is that competition is looked down upon. Students are angry because of the orchestra here, at Yale, and the fact that some people are going to be playing first flute while others won't and after all, they are here to study, and they're paying to study and they should get an equal chance, but if some people would take it as a challenge that they weren't first flute in the orchestra and go home and practice four hours on orchestra parts or whatever instead of laying down and saying, "Hurt me, I'm vulnerable," and to take the challenge as they would if they were in New York trying to get a freelance job—you'd really have to be in some shape because, if you didn't play as well as somebody else, then they would play first. This thing of being sheltered by the school . . . the school shelters you, and says, "Yes, you can sit there and play duets, play in woodwind quintets and that's okay—you don't have to learn your orchestra repertoire and you don't have to have a big tone and you can still play first when it's your turn." Well, hell, way back when Curtis produced all the orchestral players—that school turned out players who could go out and get an orchestra job. It was terribly competitive, some people don't like this kind of pressure. They think these halls of ivy must shelter everyone. But we shouldn't shelter them because reality is that when they go out no one will shelter them whatsoever. They'll be out in the cold, cruel world with just the experience they've gleaned from around here. And that's what they're going to have to live on. Some people don't like to feel second best to some other student, but unfortunately there has to be one who is second. You can't have six people all equal—all first.

P.E. I think the music schools should offer more varied opportunities for performance that would involve the students in community presentations, instead of just the concerts given within the school and for their classmates.

NYFENGER Yes, I like it when people get playing jobs with the local orchestra, the New Haven Symphony, or a concert series and learn to deal with some of the players who aren't so good sometimes or are better.

P.E. What do you mean by "players that aren't so good?" The over specialized player?

NYFENGER Yes, that's very difficult—quite hard to change because if you've gone for four years somewhere and then come here and no one says, "Look, you'd better learn to do some other things," well, it gets harder and harder to change. They get like old people. They're not willing to try anything. But I've found that with wind players, for instance, all the literature up to the last few years—I mean, if a wind player comes here and plays, how, I don't care—I don't care how many fingers they have or what kind of tone . . . I can always tell you if they know anything about harmony or if they can play the keyboard.

P.E. How can you tell?

NYFENGER By the inflection—if they obviously show no relationship in their playing to the harmonic structure. Oh, the may play the right notes and horizontally everything is connected together, but you can tell that they don't know what's going down there anywhere—then, I'm sorry—that's the one thing that I hate about some of the modern trends in the orchestra.

P.E. What do you mean by modern trends in the orchestra?

NYFENGER Well, I have found that people like Georges Laurent, or William Kincaid had a great variety of sounds in their playing and inflections according to the music that they were playing. Whereas I find that there are so many players so intent on making every note sound the same, and being so careful not to miss a note, so they won't anger the conductor.

P.E. They won't take chances.

NYFENGER Yes, and their attitude is, "I will learn all the orchestra parts in the four years I'm in school. I will practice and I will learn all those parts perfectly and will learn to play all the notes. I have no time to worry about tone quality or about changing sounds. I have no time to study any advanced harmony or learn to play the keyboard, so if someone tells me to play a little louder, then I'll do it and everything is fine." I also link it a little to dehumanization. Look into everything. Look at the changes in industry—it has changed from the craftsman to the pushing of buttons. Socially, things have changed—how certain expressions of one's feelings are not looked upon as calmly as they used to be—how people treat one another . . . all of this is reflected in the arts—so you get a very technical expression in the arts.

P.E. But how do you feel this dehumanization is expressed in performing?

NYFENGER I just had a talk with Tom Fay who is talking to everyone on the Yale faculty about what they do theoretically in their lessons and in their seminars—whether they talk about whole pieces and structure, form or do they say, "Let's just get the notes," if there is just mention of the left hand and nothing about music. For instance, I think I can play most of the flute repertoire from memory—the piano parts . . . so, if anyone comes in and says, "Nobody knows those accomplishments," well, I'd say, "Not only do I know what's going on in my head, but I can sit down and play them." I'm not going to ask you all to do that but don't you feel sort of silly playing one line of something where there is a lot more going on? An actor has to know all the parts, otherwise, if he doesn't listen, and then says his line, and doesn't relate it to the one before or after—it's terrible.

P.E. It's existentialism.

NYFENGER It's *exit*-tensialism. I'd like to go back to as much color and as much interest in playing. I'm the sort of person that I'll take a chance on some normal technical thing, an interval, to try to do something dynamically that you're not supposed to try to do and crack a note. I'd rather have that happen than get all those notes in and have it be dull! I'm not saying that I'm always going to crack notes if I try something, but it does happen. I can't play for a conductor who would say, "Tom, my god—you've ruined me. My reputation is gone because the flute cracked a note." Nowadays, I shouldn't say nowadays because it's an accumulative process, but composers write more and more difficult things and we are a little behind—so we're always catching up and working harder and harder technically. But then some people forget about taking time to learn and to figure out what the music is about. When I was nineteen, I played some chamber music with some older people and one man said, "Gee, you really get around on the flute very nicely and everything, but you have to learn about music." And I thought, "Gee, that's sort of a funny thing to say." But of course, he was right . . . at nineteen you don't know that much about music. I didn't feel terrible . . . I just thought, "It's so hard to think of it as learning about music," but then, all the things I faced after that, all the theory courses, history of music and the harmony, all the musicology—there was so much to learn and that's what he meant—except for what they call applied music. The only thing they call applied music is performance and they should call solfege and harmony applied music. Use it in a performance and you keep it in your head—do something with it instead of finding out what the progressions are and writing them down in your harmony book and then forgetting them. My biggest gripe is that there are two many monochrones going around playing important things in one tone, one line horizontally-orientated one tone players. I have always felt, if they want to do that, they should play the hammond organ or they should be pianists. They can do wonderful things with dynamics and the tone is there. A baby hits the key and gets a sound. If one doesn't want to work on tone development, then they need an instrument where they won't have to. One of my students here was getting more and more frustrated, going more and more into jazz playing and everything. He said, I'm tired of working on tone. With this amplifier I could push a button and get this huge sound—why should I work on long tones? Well, this is the thing. I could push a button and watch t.v. instead of reading. I don't want to sound paranoid but these things are happening and this trend that has come along over the last fifteen and twenty years is something we have to put pressure against, otherwise it will just envelop us.

P.E. What specific trend are you speaking of?

NYFENGER Mechanization. The antiseptic pouring of alcohol over the whole orchestra so that everything comes out clean and without too much life—so that it would be "perfect."

P.E. Who are the musicians who are putting pressure against this?

NYFENGER There is a nucleus of players in New York City and there are a couple of contractors who would rather have Henry Schuman on the oboe and myself on the flute than a few old timers or a few of the kids who just want to play notes.

P.E. How do you teach your students the different kinds of articulation?

NYFENGER Instead of suggesting to listen to another flute player I say, "Try and listen to the fifth movement of Brittin's *Serenade for Tenor, Horn and Strings*, try an oboe quartet, someone's clarinet playing for the kind of attack—if you want to hear it bright—listen—since you have to work with other players unless you're going to play unaccompanied pieces the rest of your life. You have to relate to other sonorities and through experimenting. I have found, for instance, that if a flute plays in exact unison with the violin section and plays a very bright sound—it's like another violin down there and you can't tell if it's a flute, but if you play a little more open sound—suddenly there is something added—there is the flute playing along. But if you play that open sound with oboe or the clarinet, it sounds terrible—you have to do something different—play a little brighter sound, add some more overtones to what is going on. You have to analyze the different qualities of the other instruments before you can play with them and make some sense out of it. In a woodwind quintet, I don't play the same way as I would in the orchestra.

P.E. How do you play differently?

NYFENGER I find I could play sounds in a way more compact and I'm able to move closer to a lot of articulations which are quicker on the clarinet and oboe, for instance, and to have a secondary sound when playing the harmony. You need a less focused tone to sound like the second voice to the other instruments and a more focused sound does not necessarily have to be louder than anyone else but a more soloistic sound. Now, if I'm warming up on something, I start out basically with a few tones and I try to take the sound I will need for that particular piece or that concert—which is just a generalized sound. Albert Tipton played flute duets with me once, and I said, "Gee, I didn't realize you played like that!" And he said, "Well, I don't play like that in the orchestra. It's different when I play in the orchestra."

P.E. What do you say to a student who asks you, "What should my tone sound like?"

NYFENGER Yes, they ask that often . . . but, first, everyone is different emotionally and physically and they should consider what sort of sound they would like. The problem is that the teacher makes the student in his own image and unfortunately finds that there is no one who can be in his own image—there is no one exactly like him — so what you do have are bad copies. I did a little chart of all the famous teachers I have known and you find about a dozen students who have made it from each of these teachers and you listen to them play — so, you have this one who figured that Kincaid was tone color, so he tries for the tone color but his technique isn't so good or this one thought Kincaid was stability, so he gets everything together but it's boring. I'm thinking about definite people but I wouldn't mention any names. They're still alive. Each one is a sort of partial copy, you know, one facet of this great player. Now you find one or two people who studied with other people who were teaching back then and they tried out all these things — tried out all the tone qualities they liked and put it all together and came up with what was themselves.

P.E. They arrive at their own identity. How do you memorize a piece?

NYFENGER My visual memory is terrible so I memorize by ear except for technical problems. I hear a Mozart concerto and I see it on the keyboard — the harmonic patterns and intervals. I played the piano for many years and that helps.

P.E. How do you work out a difficult passage?

NYFENGER I figure out the difficulty and take it slowly. The passage is not usually one hundred percent difficult — it's usually one or two intervals — so instead of worrying about the large interval — play what's before and after. No matter what the meter or beat is, put things into easy groups. If you have a group of sixteenths in two four time — you don't have to play four at a time to get what you want — you can use five and three and still get eight.

P.E. There are many ways to work out a problem — just use your imagination.

NYFENGER Right.

P.E. What is the ideal state of mind when performing?

NYFENGER That of being the best prepared, understanding the hall in which you're going to perform and getting past the idea that you're going to be psyched out by the audience.

P.E. How do you get past the idea of being psyched out by the audience?

NYFENGER By looking down at them or by being confident and that the audience loves me — that they are as important to the whole experience as I and that I am doing something for them and I'm not just standing there all dressed up. If you don't start out by believing in your own playing, no one else will either. At Binghamton, where I used to teach, I had a moratorium on unprepared lessons — you know, you'll always play timidly if you haven't prepared, and don't have confidence at any level. You're always aided even at the worse of times, to say, "I play very well."

P.E. Especially at auditions.

NYFENGER At auditions even more. You're trying to sell yourself to someone who doesn't have to buy you — who hasn't bought his ticket. My problem at auditions was that I had some idea of who would be listening and I'd play for them — try to please them by playing the way they liked — but that isn't good because you can't change and prepare in five seconds what you think someone else will like — you've got to present what you've prepared and then, if they ask you for something else, accomodate them — be flexible.

P.E. Maturity and artistry go hand in hand don't they?

NYFENGER I don't think people build up a personal concept of their tone and style until their thirties or forties.

P.E. How can one learn to listen to oneself and acquire objectivity?

NYFENGER I record what I play and then compare what I produce with great artists-players and see what I'm projecting. When it sounds like this — close to me, I know what it sounds like far away.

P.E. I don't understand.

NYFENGER Heifetz makes a lot of scratching noises up close but out in the audience it sounds very different. So, you see, up close you can't really judge. I have been told by students that I exaggerate too much, so I tell them, they should sit in an orchestra section and listen to all the noise and then go back to the conservatory orchestra and compare. They must play out a lot more in order to make it through a one hundred piece orchestra. But most people remain tiny copies of their teachers — they don't exaggerate at all — they only hear around their ear.

P.E. What do you demand most from your students?

NYFENGER That they know more than just their own line — to rather make mistakes than have no knowledge of their relation to the accompaniment, the orchestra or the quintet. Those who will be successful are the ones who can do it all and have a little extra knowledge — saying all the notes is not everything. I know all the accompaniments to all the pieces I do, and why they are inflected in a certain way — not just that it goes up or down. They should think about the harmonies and the rhythmic reasons for inflecting.

P.E. What does the Yale School of Music expect from its students?

NYFENGER They go along with most of what I've spoken about though the big frustration is that a lot of people feel they don't have enough time to practice because they're studying technical or historical things, but they forget that practicing will go on beyond graduation, when they will have more time. We are here to add direction and to strengthen the ensemble and orchestral programs — there is always an inequity between that and reality.

P.E. The inequity is not helped by the lack of direction about how to survive as a musician.

NYFENGER Well, for all the people with concerto and sonata aspirations, there is not enough room in the profession. Absence of pedagogical experience is not conducive to survival—most people will end up sitting in their chairs for forty years and giving a few lessons—but people should prepare to do something on a high level and players who practice orchestra parts just a week before their audition are doomed to failure.

P.E. But what of the teacher's responsibility to talk of the realities?

NYFENGER Teachers try to escape that—they play in orchestras, ensembles, when they come here. They would like to have a change so they talk about sonata and concerto, but they must also talk about orchestra parts, theory and what is relevant. I would like to have a survival plan where I could place some students in orchestras so they could se if they like it or if they don't want to do it. A doctor is working throughout his years in schools and at hospitals, so by the time he graduates he knows if he can stand the sight of blood.

P.E. While developing your tone, did you listen to string or brass instruments and try to incorporate what you heard into your playing?

NYFENGER I originally listened to a lot of instruments and since I played the double bass and played the piano . . .

P.E. I can't imagine you playing the double bass!

NYFENGER I did. I was fourth bass in the All City High School Orchestra in Cleveland—that's like being at home plate—fourth base, you know? Out of eight or so . . . but it was a good experience to find out how the strings worked and I studied some conducting and the bass helped to know about bowing. I remember going to the Cleveland Orchestra concerts and particularly paying attention to Mark Lifshly, the first oboist, who was a real artist and had shapes to his sound which flutists usually don't have.

P.E. What kind of shapes did he have in his sound?

NYFENGER He had a lot of strange sort of shapes . . . rounding off notes and a lot of changes of color in vibrato that I thought were really interesting so I paid a lot of attention to him. And, also, to Robert Marcellus, the first clarinetist, who is very clear and has the kind of attack that we wish we had on the flute. Later, I got very interested in analogies between strings and winds—and I'm writing a book about it now. The strings have had such a headstart on us in terms of repertoire, control of dynamics—without going out of tune, and in terms of phrase endings—that it seemed to me to be a good idea to try to study those.

P.E. What string players did you listen to?

NYFENGER I listened to a lot of string players also in conjunction with singers. Now I tell a student, that even if they don't have a great voice, to sing the phrase and you find that they end the note much more easily than they do on their instrument. They should make the instrument do that. Your voice is inside of you all your life and you can control it. On the violin, on the other hand, you slow down the bow and the tone gets smaller or softer but the pitch remains correct. We're afraid at times to do good phrase endings because our pitch is lost—so we have to work at it.

P.E. What do you look for in a singer's phrase endings?

NYFENGER The different roundings off at different speeds, for instance, the voice is unlikely to do an eighth note that cuts off abruptly. There is a bell-like quality to the end and it doesn't end upward—so that a half note can take in a long range of dynamics from beginning to end but an eighth note can encompass the same range. An eighth note will end and sound very human and not chopped off—not strangled. So, the winds are only in the beginning of efforts at really doing it well. Whereas we didn't try to before. Even vibrato came late. The strings had it for a couple of centuries and we didn't have it until this century.

P.E. How have you begun to organize your book? Do you have a title yet? How did you begin?

NYFENGER I started with looking at all the books that tried to give instructions of beginning pieces—of beginning etudes and I found that there is plenty of material of this sort but down to earth works that had analogies seemed to be missing, so I wound up calling it *Flute Prescriptions and Analogies*. Prescriptions for all different problems, for example, the ways of looking into these problems and analogies using the other instruments and the voice to find a way to do these things. Because, for instance, when you try to tell someone to do a certain thing with the air, you can't see it, but you can show them how the violin bow does it. And then they get an idea what it's about and then they can incorporate it and make the air do what they see the violin bow doing. And there are analogies between every day things . . . the walking procedure of a human being where there are definite steps but there is motion in between—anything like that to help with musical ideas. So in the first part of the book I talk about all the different problems and some of the analogies and in the second part—how to work at these things and the third part shows how to apply them to pieces.

P.E. What pieces have you chosen?

NYFENGER I've even chosen some string pieces and some clarinet pieces to show that without vibrato we could phrase. That as Moyse says, "Vibrato hides the misery of your bad phrasing sometimes." In order to play a Mozart clarinet concerto, make the notes stick together in the way the clarinet does and then perhaps you can use a little vibrato now and then.

P.E. You feel players use too much vibrato?

NYFENGER Well, it becomes like the constant of the Hammond organ where you just turn the switch and you just vibrate all the time. I hate to have my students do this. Because, if dynamics are color, and you don't play different dynamics—you've lost something and if different endings of notes are color and if you make every ending the same, you've lost something, and if you vibrate beautifully, but all the time, it is no longer a color. It's a constant—"o o o o o o," and you're stuck. So it becomes like working in a shop—you're craftsman but no artist.

P.E. What other things do you listen for in singers besides the rounding of ends of phrases?

NYFENGER Certainly, there is articulation. For instance, if one were to play the Schubert *Introduction to Variations* which is from a song, when you hear the words and when you hear the articulations, it changes the way you play on the flute. You have to work it over again, once you've heard the voice. If you hear Fischer-Diskeau sing it, then you know you've heard something pretty good and you have to reevaluate.

P.E. Say you listen to Fischer-Diskeau or Peter Pears sing a Schubert song, how do you begin to approximate what they did in your playing?

NYFENGER Well, some of the beginning consonants of words can denote a stronger attack. You can also hear different pulses — not that you can always use the consonants and vowels because you may not be able to keep a line, but you can certainly hear a difference between them. The natural use of vibrato which is not always constant in a voice . . . when someone tells me that I had a vocal vibrato, I'm most happy or if they tell me I sound more like the violin, I'm most happy because these are instruments with a natural resonance. When you take the bow off the string, there is still a sound, but when you stop blowing on the flute, it's dead, you have to approximate the ending, you have to make it.

P.E. To approximate the ending, do you build from your toes up, from the earth up?

NYFENGER It's a nice thought. Also, you build away from the flute — when it feels right — when everything has been analyzed and worked out and practiced — then I like to feel like the flute is gone. I don't have to tell the fingers anymore. I don't have to tell the position to the lips. Then it begins to work.

P.E. You're still working on this?

NYFENGER I'll always be working on this. And when I finish working on it — then I'll be very old. If I stop NOW, I'd be very old now. When you're through improving — you're through. I won't mention who but there is someone with the same vibrato for sixty-five years or so. Another person, like Kincaid or Julius Baker or Rampal — was sounding the same through their career but finding new things and learning even from their students — studying with them. I heard a marvelous young girl who came in to play for the graduate school and she had certain things she was doing in a piece that I never thought of and she's only twenty-two. So I ran to my little studio after she played and I tried to do what she did. There is nothing wrong with that. And I would hope that when I'm fifty, if I told someone everything that I had figured out, by the time they were twenty-three or thirty, they would play better than I do. There is no room to be selfish. They should be better than I am. Everything should improve as in athletics. The speeds get faster, the players get stronger. Any football athlete will admit that maybe he had to do more plays when he was playing football but he will say that the players now are stronger and faster. They don't kid themselves into thinking that things don't improve. The good old days were good for themselves but they are

better now.

P.E. What are some student pieces that a beginning flute student could look at?

NYFENGER Certainly the Schubert songs would be very nice — the Schubert *Shepherd on the Rock* — the clarinet part. To listen to all the clarinet phrases and try to play without vibrato for most of it and then see how it works. Especially the ability to diminuendo in going up and relax and not feel it's a strain. The string pieces, not for a beginner certainly, but an unaccompanied part that's not for the flute but which has been transcribed, Paganini's *Caprices*, which are difficult but there are also slow movements. Pieces by Saint-Saens — thematic material from violin concertos. The Romantic Period was pretty much a waste of time for the flute because the composers got into chromaticism and a lot of dynamics. The flute had a bad scale, it didn't vibrate yet, it went out of tune easily and so we were properly rejected . .by Brahms, Schumann, Liszt, Tchaikovsky — you don't hear nonorchestral flute solos by them because they didn't like the instrument. Now, if we go back and take repertoire they did — the Franck violin sonata has been transcribed now for flute and it works very well. When we take some of these pieces and use our new skills, we feel that we are doing them justice now because we can play them as musically as the violin. This is a great learning experience. cause we can play them as musically as the violin. This is a great learning experience.

P.E. Do you use the air differently when you don't want to have too much vibrato?

NYFENGER The vibrato should be within the sound but the idea of the throat having any control of the pulse of the air has to be gotten rid of, so the throat stops. Just as you would sing a long note with no vibrato — you wouldn't move it. There is really a difference of support. Some people find that when they first stop playing vibrato they drop to the bottom of their range because vibrato is also dynamics, you know, louder and softer. They find that they have to play only softer — that they can't push because they are using their throat to help the pulse of the air, which isn't so good to do all the time. There is a function in the throat — a vibrato, which people think that they could vibrate from down here but they are not fast enough — it's still up here in the throat. But, to think that you can't play a note when you are not doing that — that when you turn off your vibrato you lose your tone is a terrible thing. It would be like saying that when you stop wiggling your left hand on the violin that you couldn't bow a string.

P.E. Where does the tone come from?

NYFENGER I think that the tradition of breathing and how the whole mechanism works was best handed down to Mrs. Dwyer who talks about not using the stomach muscles by pushing them in too hard because that pushes the air up so fast that you have to tighten your throat and of using the natural rhythm inside the diaphragm muscle, and just the natural collapse of the insides because we don't really need a lot of air pressure. We don't, on the flute, have anything to blow against. We don't have a reed to hold the air back or a mouthpiece — we have to open our lips. If we blow too hard, then the lips have to squeeze the air down and that makes a tiny tone. I figured out later in life that one didn't have to push so hard or hold the lips so tightly — then you get more range of sound. Your abdominal muscles are so large compared to your poor little lip, that if you push in hard, you have to tighten your throat or your lip or both, to keep all that pressure back, and then you feel all constricted and you try to use your lip to make a tone and intervals and you have nothing left. So many players do this.

P.E. Playing like this weakens endurance.

NYFENGER It takes away from color too. If you are busy pushing the air the wrong way or tightening up your face or your throat, then you can't change the sound.

P.E. What are the different requirements of playing between the recording studio and the concert hall in regards to tone, projection and endurance?

NYFENGER That is a very good question, because I could take a very fine student into the recording studio and they could fail. They might breathe too loudly for a recording for background music for film or commercial things. I just did eleven and a half hours for something. But for these things where the composer has no time to rehearse everything, to control the dynamics — a microphone is stuck within inches of you and learning how to play, in the manner that Julius Baker learned how to play so successfully, is to practice with microphones and figure it out. To cut out the high frequencies and the hardness of the sound that you would use in the concert hall and to use a slightly smaller but very flexible rounded sound. Also by turning up the volume electronically you can make a huge, big sound.

P.E. So you don't play full before the microphone?

NYFENGER Except when they ask you to. Now another kind of session, say a *Mostly Mozart* Festival recording I did recently, the microphones would be about six or eight feet away with a couple microphones covering the wind section. Now I can play almost the normal way and when I go back and listen, if it is too edgy, I might modify it a little bit. In the concert hall, I will exaggerate just as an actor exaggerates in projecting his voice when you hear the consonants and you see the spit go across the room but he knows that he is reaching the audience properly. The sound may have a lot of scratch in it, as I said before, and the young players are afraid of this. They should all go and listen to Heifetz or Rostropovitch or someone like that up close and realize how much scratch there is and the beauty of the sound in the hall. They are afraid of that noise up close and actually the flute embouchure is inches from your ear and they hear the sound of the air and are afraid but they should learn not to be.

P.E. They want to hear it like the audience should hear it.

NYFENGER They are selfish if they do that. I tell them that they are closet players. They are playing only for themselves. They are not professional. You have to play for the people out there. On the other hand, for a recording, I have demonstrated with a good microphone that I could play between pianissimo and mezzo piano and make the whole range but some people will say that this is dishonest. But the result is that you are making a record.

P.E. Why would they say it is dishonest?

NYFENGER Because this is not how you would sound in the hall. Because you are using electronic things and you are cutting off some of those kinds of sounds you use. But I have come to the conclusion that if I make a recording and it is beautiful and if I play it in a concert and it doesn't sound like that in the twentieth row — that's too bad. They should understand that it is not the same. Some people — some artists• become paranoid and won't play a concert anymore or won't make a record anymore — you don't have to go to this extreme.

P.E. Are there any more specific things to keep in mind about the differences in projection?

NYFENGER Well, specifically by blowing everything softer through a smaller embouchure opening between the lips and perhaps the flute turned back slightly to darken the sound so that the bright overtones won't sound harsh up close — I think that's mainly it, and also you may hear occasionally a recording where a wind player seems to play forever on one breath and then he plays a concert and he has to take two extra breaths in that phrase — that's because he was able to play it softly for the recording and it was amplified.

P.E. Why does he have to take the two extra breaths?

NYFENGER Because you use up more air playing loudly. On the other hand, the microphones being a lot like the ear — since they are like the ear, it's like having a person in the audience standing withing six inches with his ear towards you, you know you wouldn't want to play as you would in a concert hall with that feeling of a person standing there that close. That's the way I play. A person's ear is there and it's going to be coming out anyway through the speakers. So I don't want to offend them with the sound. Whereas when they are sitting twelve feet away, I don't think this way.

P.E. In the concert hall, have you ever played with a microphone — some amplification?

NYFENGER No, I don't. No. If it is slightly amplified like Philharmonic Hall on a certain occasion, the microphone is likely to be twelve feet away so I am not worried about it.

P.E. How do you think differently in the concert hall? Like an actor do you think of the last row — the back wall?

NYFENGER I think of the sound ringing and I try out the stage and rehearse — and if I don't hear anything coming back from the end of my note, then it is the wrong tone for the place. I have to play very brightly in Philharmonic Hall, with the high ceiling and not much surrounding you to project out, but in Alice Tully Hall and Carnegie Recital Hall, I play a little less brightly.

P.E. Is it a good idea to check out the hall ... with different headjoints?

NYFENGER Right. I've tried out a flute with a platinum headjoint and a gold flute for a specific concert and a lady I was with at the concert who has a very good ear went out and listened to the two flutes and said that the platinum headjoint was big and full but the gold flute was really nice but wasn't making it. Then the hall filled up with people and I played the first piece on the platinum headjoint — it was nice but it seemed to be a little bit dead. So I played the gold flute for the second half and I felt more sound, therefore I was deceived — which I shouldn't have been, but not having the gold flute for very long I should have realized that the brightness was going to be absorbed when the people came in, so what was left of the brightness in the platinum flute was absorbed and didn't project as far as it should have. No one said it was bad, they all said that the gold flute had more sound. Sometimes I'll practice playing very brightly and play in one of these cavernous places like a museum or hall that is so bright that the gold flute or that kind of sound seems to me to be inappropriate — if I rehearse, then I'll change back to the other. Of course, within the player there is a change too. The player — no matter what instrument you play, can still change the sound. You don't have to just change instruments.

P.E. How would you change the sound?

NYFENGER Change the angle or blowing — or the amount of intensity.

P.E. What kind of flute do you use in recording — silver, platinum or gold?

NYFENGER I have used the platinum but recently I've been using the gold flute because it's still very heavy metal and resistant and it doesn't tend toward a lot of buzzy sound. The silver might be described as a general all around sound and then the gold would lean toward, as some people say, the sound of the sunlight — a certain warmth, and the platinum tends to give a center, which the other two don't give for me, more of a masculine sound.

P.E. You played in Arthur Weisberg's group. Since you were playing new music, did your concept of playing change in regards to color or phrasing?

NYFENGER I was chasing after each new piece and the new ideas that each person had. And searching around ... I had played in a group which was also contemporary before for a few years, so it wasn't all brand new. I was looking for ways to do the contrasting dynamics and looking for sounds that were appropriate. Someone would come up with a new sound or effect and you would have to try to work it out.

P.E. Did you ever find yourself doing something that you thought you couldn't? That you never expected to do and did that remain constant in your playing? Did it change your playing?

NYFENGER Oh, when you're restretching limits of range and limits of color, you find that some of it spills over to normal, old repertoire too.

P.E. You weren't afraid of that? Some flutists are.

NYFENGER No, I was afraid of blowing myself out. Of trying to do all these things and then having the same day to play something else ... and although they say that if you're relaxed it shouldn't happen, if you do six hours of contemporary music that you should still be able to go back and play a Bach sonata, I never found it quite true. It would take me a day or so to change back. Maybe that was my own trouble but I have always had that problem.

P.E. But the problem never kept you from having that experience?

NYFENGER No. It was just frustrating sometimes.

P.E. Did playing new music change your way of practising?

NYFENGER Yes, especially how to warm up.

P.E. In what way?

NYFENGER Well, you can have a well tuned up body but if you are warming up for a track event, it's different than if you are warming up for wrestling. So, if this was a concert for flute, piccolo and alto flute all in one concert and a lot of dynamic range, you would have to warm up as a doubler would. One instrument for awhile, then another instrument, then another instrument for awhile. You would try out different effects spending a few minutes on each instrument, a few seconds and then jumping back and forth. The important thing about a warm up is to incorporate all the things that are going to happen in the piece.

P.E. You work from the pieces?

NYFENGER Yes. Going over different things slowly before and when you find that you are not doing the usual triads and scales — that the pieces are not so accessible from your old experience, you have to warm up and practice more carefully than you did before.

P.E. You mentioned having a well tuned body. Do you do any exercise, yoga or diet?

NYFENGER Well, after I successfully missed the Korean War because of a bad back, I took to some exercises to try to fix it. And on and off, I run because that's good for the wind, but I also find it's good for catching cold in the winter — so I tried to lift some weights and I played tennis until I had my eye accident three years ago — it's very hard to judge the speed of a ball with one eye. Being in condition is very important ... Mr. Kincaid and his swimming and Baker jogging.

P.E. Do you smoke?

NYFENGER No, I think that's terrible. I think it's great to exercise but I become very lazy during the teaching session. I say I'm going to exercise but after a long day I don't. I'm at the ripe young age of thirty-nine and it's very easy to get a big stomach — and that wouldn't be so good for me. Some people say, "Look at all the players with stomachs and they feel better when they play." But they also come off stage panting sometimes from the effort. I would rather not have that. Barring laziness, I do get to do some exercise — I did some this morning.

P.E. What did you do?

NYFENGER I did a few sit ups, a few weights to align the vertebrae and all. As far as meditation goes, I tried a few things and being very hyper — I find that at times sitting very quietly and forgetting about students is a great boon to the nervous system.

P.E. How about your scrubbing the floor at six-thirty this morning?

NYFENGER Oh, yes. While other people were doing their snoring tones carefully — I was scrubbing the floor. I haven't been able to sleep too well — so I get up at four in the morning sometimes.

P.E. If you were the dean of a music school, how would you structure the music education for a flutist or any instrumentalist?

NYFENGER Well, as the dean, when they were born I would start playing records at home and when they told me that they wanted to go on with it, I would have a piano they could pick away at — like I did. So they could see how the notes worked, what the intervals are and after they figured out how to play the piano formally a little bit — then they could play another instrument. I think we're a little backwards here because we are just picking up the European idea of theoretical education for little kids now. But the other answer to the question would be that reflecting a professional situation is very important. People really believe that after they get out of school that they will suddenly develop a professional attitude because they will have to and it seldom works. Being close to professional people who are teachers and being made to be aware of the kind of work you have to do — like being on time, spending a certain amount of time thinking about pieces instead of waiting until it's too late to do these things are very important. As far as course structures, people take theoretical subjects very lightly until they go into a recording studio and someone says, "I'd like a half diminished seventh there — up and down on C for a couple of bars just to fill in," and they don't know what the person is talking about. They suddenly wished they had paid attention in theory. One girl just played for me beautifully and I said, "You play piano don't you?" And she said, "Yes." Then I said, "You play some other instrument." And she said, "The violin." She was playing the flute like the violin sometimes. Some of the problems that come into a college start at birth when the child hasn't been able to listen to things, and takes up the instrument very late and doesn't do any theory and instead of trying to fix these basic things at a college level, they should be started much earlier. Instead of coming across the doorstep and becoming a problem to the faculty. Now, I only accept people who are good at these things and can talk about music. It may sound cruel, but just because they can move their fingers around doesn't mean they're going to be successful in grad school. You see, most theory study should have been done before but it's always possible to take more courses in even peripheral subjects and analysis and if someone says they've done all sorts of figured solfege — well, let them do keyboard harmony or play things from bass or whatever.

P.E. What is the most important thing a teacher could do for his student in graduate school?

NYFENGER To find out what's missing and not to take the student too seriously — their evaluation too seriously. Like when they say, "I don't think I want to do this." I think it's negotiable but I think we can be too lenient and say, "Okay, then we'll just practice this year and take one course in Afro-European linguistics." And then three years later, they're asking you what goes on in a piece of music — but it's too late. I still believe that it can be individualized very much. People don't have to be shoved into one big course. If someone can sight sing in seven clefs but can't play the piano — then he should learn to play the piano.

P.E. You would like a more personal program rather than a general blueprint.

NYFENGER You could have the same ends — you could say that there are going to be examinations someday or orals but if someone is deficient in one thing — that's the thing they're going to have to work on. People should not be just lumped together. In performance, it appears, even though we don't take care of — bouncing out the dive of performers, that the ones who have the ambition can do it themselves. They find groups and things to do as players. Those who sit around and mope about not having anything to do . . .

P.E. Are expecting you to do it.

NYFENGER Want someone to do it for them. "So and so doesn't like me so he doesn't get me any jobs." While you are spending time thinking about that — you can spend some time figuring out how you're playing.

P.E. What is your definition of a professional attitude, besides being on time?

NYFENGER Cooperation. It is slightly different from the attitude of a visual artist.

P.E. How is it different?

NYFENGER A visual artist looks at something later and says, "I don't like this — I'll change it." But when you have ten people doing it at once . . .

P.E. But have you been in a situation where you have believed in playing a note or a phrase differently from your colleagues?

NYFENGER Sure. But there is such a thing as saying, "I don't agree with that, but I'll do it." If that's bad though, you better change your situation. In New York, there are some conductors who are exceptional cripples — as far as what they know about music, but they manage to get a concert or two at a certain point in life. You can say, "Sir, if I have to play that, it will be ugly. I don't want to play that." You can have an argument with this person and if you have the argument properly — the next engagement the player is back and the conductor isn't or, if that conductor is back for something, you don't have to accept the job. On the other hand, if you are going to play in an orchestra which is controlled by a certain conductor — you wouldn't accept the position unless you know you'll get along. If you want to be subservient, then collect your money and spend it all on ulcer medicine.

P.E. How about when you play commercial jobs?

NYFENGER Certainly, one can go in and do some commercial jobs where you may neither agree with the company nor the person who wrote the commercial but you see how much money you're going to get — and your name won't be used . . . so whether your integrity has been ruffled . . .

P.E. No one knows. Is graduate school the time to learn — strengthen the professional attitude?

NYFENGER That's the time to learn it.

P.E. You don't think they should already have it?

NYFENGER Some people will have it when they are twelve. Others will take a long time. I had this great experience of going back and seeing the people in my graduating class in college. People who were always late and who were not very responsible — even the ones who played fairly well . . . none were playing. They had all lost it and were doing something else. Selling insurance or teaching somewhere. They thought they would learn the professional attitude when they graduated but they couldn't shift gears — they couldn't get along. They thought they could change — but they were not able to change. That's why I tell people now — don't say, "Well, I'll start coming on time when I get out of school," because you won't be able to.

P.E. How would you like to structure your career from here on? What would you like to be doing most?

NYFENGER I have been dissatisfied with sitting in the orchestra pit for the ballet for five years. At first, it seemed to be a lifetime's work and the security became more important with a growing family and whereas I started out playing in New York doing freelance things and then playing in chamber groups simultaneously with the Contemporary Ensemble and the ballet and then just a few students here and there, that when the Contemporary Ensemble ended, I found myself looking towards Yale for more work and then, when I didn't want to do the ballet anymore, I took another day at Yale and Vassar and little by little I was mostly teaching. The New York Woodwind Quintet plays a few concerts and I do a few things with Midnight Bach and the Mostly Mozart Festival during the summers. I've gotten away from playing a lot. Also, it's difficult to practice after listening to eight hours worth of students. But now I'm changing my life this next year with the four day appointment here at Yale and giving up going to Vassar and giving up one of the days I go to New York so I should have more time to practice. I have an offer to make a recording — so I'll do that. A few people want me to give some master classes so I'll do those and now as I'm going to turn forty — I'll have a little time to play. I started out playing a lot in my twenties, then I slowed down and now I'm going to start up again. I hope my career will combine some lecturing, talking to students and having recitals. I don't see taking over the recital world and just travelling around. My travels will be very much connected with teaching but

not on the basis of giving one to one lessons.

P.E. Would you ever give up teaching?

NYFENGER No.

P.E. Why?

NYFENGER Gee, I could say that it makes me feel important. It does! I feel important because I feel I know what I am talking about and that people, for the most part, appreciate it. Teaching dies if it doesn't go on. The audience comes from it. If I have a couple dozen students and then they are out teaching and showing people and making them interested in music and then they come to concerts and their friends come to concerts — you are already doing something for playing . . . just from teaching. All the playing that Rampal has done and all the classes he's taught have made the flute very popular. If no one teaches, then no one plays or studies with them. I feel that if I don't communicate verbally then something is lost in my playing. Sometimes I learn by talking to a student. I'll say, "Do this!". Then I'll try it myself after they've gone through the door and I look to make sure they've gone before I try it! Also, I learn from my very good students — those who have created something themselves. Studying *with* is the word. Taking from has to go. You don't take from them and they don't take from you. Stealing! That's what it's called!

P.E. What flutists had a large influence on you?

NYFENGER My grand teacher Kincaid — he's a lot of people's grand teacher. And certainly Maurice Sharp who's first chair in the Cleveland Orchestra and was my teacher while I was there. But I would like to think that all the hours I studied with Baker without paying him and with Rampal without paying him — you know, from the records and all the different styles and directions like Albert Tipton's perfectionism, and the expansiveness of Mrs. Dwyer's playing in the orchestra — countless other people.

P.E. Do you play along with the records?

NYFENGER I don't usually play along with them — I play after them. I like to be a good mimic. I think it's a sign of respect. I don't think I play like any of them now, but if you do a genealogy of good players, you'll find that there aren't many who studied with just one person. You have to take examples from a lot of things to find your own thing.

P.E. What do you feel when you're playing music out there? Do you know?

NYFENGER Yes. If I feel in communication with the audience, or in communion with the audience — then I'm not frightened. And I feel that they're supporting me and want me to do something well. I feel as if my arms were around them and they are all up close and I feel . . . large — when things are right. But when I'm more nervous I don't feel quite as large but you have to get through it anyway. That's the professional attitude. But at the Midnight Bach Concerts, when people don't come just to show off their mink coats but come to hear me play, that's pretty nice. There is an inspiration and things get a little bit bigger. The sound gets bigger and the phrasing gets more magnanimous. There is a difference between the concert hall and your studio — when your knees don't shake too much but you have to love yourself or use your imagination.

MURRAY PANITZ

MURRAY PANITZ

Murray Panitz was born in New York. He is a graduate of the Eastman School of Music where he studied with Joseph Mariano and the Manhattan School of Music. He attended the Juilliard Summer School where he studied with Arthur Lora. He has a masters degree in theory. He was the principal flutist in the National Symphony of Washington before joining the Air Force after which he decided to go to New York. There, he held various non-musical jobs while earning a masters degree in theory under the G.I. Bill. He became a successful freelancer and was the first flutist with the New York City Ballet and the Little Orchestra Society of New York and with such major recording orchestras as MGM, Decca, Capitol, RCA and the Columbia Recording Orchestra.

In 1961, he joined the Philadelphia Orchestra as first flutist and is currently on the faculties of Temple University and the Curtis Institute of Music.

With the Philadelphia Orchestra, he has travelled to China during Mao Tse-tung's reign.

Mr. Panitz has appeared for two seasons with the Casals Festival in Puerto Rico and has toured the Mediterranean with the Philadelphia Woodwind Quintet. He has given solo performances in New York, Saigon and Hong Kong.

He lives in Cherry Hill, New Jersey with his wife and daughter. When he has time, he likes to read.

SETTING

George Raft and Murray Panitz could have played a game of poker and called it a contest. Men who hold the cards close to their chests, accept the rules of the game and know how to wait to win.

"I never thought of losing," he said drawing on his cigarette while sitting on a green sofa with a metallic gold pillow with gold tassels at the other end. "A lot of it is luck. You have to be in the right place at the right time, without that, all the playing is secondary," and he throws up a hand with fine, long fingers.

Our dialogue does not run face to face yet, for he is slightly turned away, his legs crossed, his chin lowered, grazing his big chest and his handsome face in profile, but when he does face me, the dark, bright eyes are intelligent, and bold yet revealing a gentleness and shy intensity.

"A drink?," he asks, swirling the ice in his. I ask for soda and he gets up tall and walks out.

His home studio in Cherry Hill, New Jersey is meticulous. Life is organized. Hung are black and white framed pictures of Eugene Ormandy in shirt sleeves conducting the Philadelphia Orchestra in rehearsal, on tables, various electronic equipment: a cassette, stereo, and microphones protected by plastic. Various music books, a paperback on Moses, James Michner's *Iberia*, Greek Mythology for reference, a bust of Beethoven, the Gregorian Chant above the sofa and music stands are placed next to a floor lamp which is lit since the beige draperies are drawn against the rainy October afternoon.

"You could use my cassette, if you have trouble with yours," he offers, handing me my drink. I thank him and place my cassette between us. He waits, drawing quick on his cigarette. I sense an oblique start is best and he laughs surprised when I say, "I don't know a thing about you."

I had met with Mr. Panitz once before at Carnegie Hall in New York. Waiting to meet me on the steps of the backstage entrance, in a trench coat and with his flute under his arm, we shook hands and decided to talk in the Maestro's dressing room, the only quiet place.

We had not been able to finish our conversation, for curtain time neared and a man opened the door and greeted Mr. Panitz with "Hello, Maestro." "I am not the Maestro." "Oh," said the man and seeing the cassette said, "You'd better hide it. If one of the Union guys see it, there will be hell to pay. No recording on the premises."

"It's my interview," said Mr. Panitz and the man closed the door.

"I'll take them as they come."

INTERVIEW

P.E. I don't know a thing about you. Only that you are the first flutist of the Philadelphia Orchestra and that you studied at the Eastman School of Music with Joseph Mariano.

PANITZ I had only five lessons with Joseph Mariano. He was the best — a prince of a person. We used to go out and drink beer — on him.

P.E. Was the flute your first instrument?

PANITZ I was a pianist and I went to the High School of Music and Art in New York City when it was just starting. At that time, every pianist had to take a secondary instrument so a teacher said to me, "You'll take the flute," and that was it. I was given a flute and although I wasn't interested in it at the start, by the time I finished my junior year in high school I decided I would become a flutist.

P.E. What changed your mind about the flute?

PANITZ I liked it because you could do more with one note than you could on the piano. It came easily to me. My teacher, at the time, was a clarinetist, and he had taught me many wrong fingerings. I found this out later when I started to study with Arthur Lora at the Juilliard Summer School. He was amazed that I was getting as many notes out of the flute as I was, with the wrong fingerings, but since I have a good ear, I would do all kinds of manipulations to make a pitch.

P.E. You were never too traditional from the start.

PANITZ Never. I don't observe tradition much. Even my teaching is somewhat non-traditional. I don't use a method of any sort. Having a good teacher is an important asset, if he is good, it's a help; if he is not, then you have to use your own mentality to learn.

P.E. Did you set goals for yourself early in your career?

PANITZ At the outset, I decided that I wanted to be the first flutist of the Philadelphia Orchestra. That was the one and only goal that I had set for myself and it came to pass — which is a wonderful feeling.

P.E. Besides being talented, ambitious, and hard working, how did your break happen?

PANITZ Partially luck. You have to have luck and be at the right place at the right time. The first time I went to audition — I didn't get the job. The second time, in 1960, I was supposed to have been in Spoleto but my wife had gotten ill and therefore I was available at home. When I first got out of college, I immediately joined the National Symphony of Washington as first flutist but I was only there for a short time because then I was called into the Air Force and when I got out of the Air Force, I decided not to go back to the National Symphony and instead went to New York.

P.E. How did you survive in New York?

PANITZ I sold records but I wasn't a very good salesman. Then I tried paper boxes and twine but I didn't sell too much of those. While I was in New York, I got a masters degree in theory with a subsidy from the government — which helped us eat. Then slowly, with luck,

things began to change. I went to auditions, when they let me audition, and I went to personnel managers and contractors and was told to fill out forms — nobody really listened to me. One guy said to me, "Why should I hire you? Even if you're the Heifetz of the flute, I've been working with the same guy for twenty years and I'm satisfied." I admired and respected his loyalty but it didn't help me. My break came when one of the big shot contractors was walking down the street, with an oboist who worked for him and who was also a friend of mine. The contractor said he needed a flute player for a Broadway engagement. He had used up his list of flutists and no one was available. My friend said to him, "Why don't you try Murray Panitz?" I was tried and that was my first entree into the musical scene. If they see you play the job and you do well, you go on to the next one. By the time I left New York, I was very successful as a freelance player. I joined the Little Orchestra Society as first flutist under Thomas Sherman then the City Center Ballet Orchestra. I played with the recording orchestras — MGM, Decca, Capitol, RCA, and the Columbia Recording Orchestra. I got lucky after a period of being unlucky.

P.E. Were you ever discouraged?

PANITZ I never thought of losing. Especially since one of my first teachers told me not to become a flutist. I was a cocky kid and I thought, "Maybe he didn't make it but I'm going to make it." A lot of it is luck — you have to be in the right place at the right time, without that, all the playing is secondary. I was available at the right time. There are times when many decisions are necessary. I have been offered positions in out of town orchestras which I have turned down. People sometimes make decisions and then grieve the day that they did because things didn't turn out right. But that's like crying over a bad draw in a poker hand. It is good to make your own decisions. I wasn't asked to spend four years in the Air Force. I had no choice. You can't be unhappy over the cards you draw. If you become unhappy, you become a cynic.

P.E. You were cocky and you believed in yourself.

PANITZ We all have an ego. But if you think too much of yourself — your ego is misplaced. You have to be able to evaluate yourself. Here you are up against one hundred flute players. If you don't put the correct evaluation on yourself, if you say, "Well, a hundred of those players play better than I do," then you're still bucking the tide, but if you could listen to the hundred and say, "I think they are pretty good, but I think I play as well as the first five or six," if you could legitimately do that, then I imagine you will feel good about yourself and you will be able to wait.

P.E. How do you best prepare your students for auditions?

PANITZ By telling them to get as much experience as they can. To study as much orchestral music as they can. To listen to it. In that way if they have to sight read, they will have an idea of the emotional content of the music and they will read a little more into the notes. The notes and technique are basically an equalizer — not too many people are going to reflect on whether the technique is a little smoother or the legato is a little better — as long as the notes come out, not too many people are aware of that. If the student has an understanding of the music, he stands a better chance. The problem is that there are too many players and not enough jobs. There aren't too many places to get experience. It is a difficult profession and it always has been. I tell people to hedge their bet a little bit. Cover yourself in another way. I wanted to be a flute player but I also took my degree in theory. Some people don't agree with this. Some say, that if you are going to try, you should try all the way. I figured I would do both. Luckily, I fulfilled my ambition. Otherwise, I would have been a theory teacher.

P.E. You seem to be a stoic.

PANITZ I have certain spartan capabilities, a high threshold of pain and am a little fatalistic. I make my own fate—to a degree. I don't blame anybody or anything for what happens to me, if I have disappointments, or if I have good luck—it's good luck and if it's bad luck—it's my bad luck. I'm prepared to live with the decision. I have made the decision with the greatest thought that I could give the situation and I have to live with it. In the same manner, I don't try to dissuade people from becoming flute players. As I said, one of my first teachers told me that I should not be a flute player—he will remain nameless, but I do feel that someone should forewarn them in advance. This is a difficult profession and one has to be prepared. They shouldn't go into it with lights in their eyes saying, "I am going to make it." They should be prepared to know that there are lots of people who are trying to make it and only one out of so many is going to.

P.E. How do you help your students acquire a sense of value of one's worth?

PANITZ I'd say, go and listen to other players and make an honest evaluation and don't be snowed by the fact that someone has a so called reputation and that you are only a student. There are students who can play better than some professionals. There is an ipso facto sort of thing, which is, that if you are first flutist of a famous orchestra, you have to be a great flutist. Hopefully, yes, but not necessarily true. Who can tell? I don't know how my colleagues will feel about this. I try to tell my students to dis-believe, and to question and not to take something as gospel. Don't hesitate to question, and experiment to find out what works best for them.

P.E. How do you structure your life?

PANITZ I am easy going. Actually, doing the freelance work in New York was more difficult than playing in the orchestra because we have a more or less set schedule so I have some time to myself. I like to read or just relax and do nothing. Teaching does get to be difficult sometimes — when our orchestra schedule gets a little heavy. Basically I stay healthy and fit. I am the world's strongest flute player. I exercise a lot.

P.E. What do you do to stay fit?

PANITZ I row in my basement with an Exerow machine. I put on the T.V. and let the time go by.

P.E. What kind of hold do you have on your flute while playing?

PANITZ Very light—from the chin to the fingers.

P.E. I read that you paste a piece of paper on the embouchure. Why do you do that?

PANITZ Because I use very little pressure against the chin. If one perspires, it is probable that you may start to press more, therefore, it enables me to hang the flute on the lip rather than digging in. I am never without it.

P.E. How does pressing a piece of paper on the embouchure help your playing?

PANITZ It gives my playing flexibility and I can vary the embouchure more. Try speaking with the flute pressed into your chin and your speech is affected. If you relax the pressure, there is no change in the speech pattern. Therefore, you can use both lips. It's better for intonation changes and control of sound.

P.E. You're working for overall relaxation?

PANITZ Yes. I don't look like I am working. The only part that works is my blowing. I take a deep breath and control it. This talk about breath control does not have to do with physical capacity. I do play some quite long phrases. It isn't because I have a greater capacity than anybody else. As a matter of fact, I have been tested, and I have just normal capacity. It's a question of controlling it, desiring it and trying to make the long phrase.

P.E. You say your capacity has been tested?

PANITZ Yes. There is a machine that measures how many liters of air you can hold. I registered in a course at the "Y." There were two doctors who examined me before the test. I thought the doctor would be amazed because I do *Afternoon of a Faun* in one breath, at a slow tempo, but he didn't blink an eyelash. I asked him about it and he said, "No, YOUR CAPACITY IS NORMAL FOR YOUR SIZE. You just have better control."

P.E. How have you developed the control?

PANITZ By playing games in the practice room. I never liked to practice too much, so when I was in the practice room, I would keep myself amused sometimes by taking out my watch to see how long I could keep a sound going. If I could do a minute, could I do a minute and five seconds? A minute and ten seconds? At one time, I was able to do small extended sounds for about a minute and forty seconds. It was a game. From that point on, I was investigating the whole area more thoroughly and I came up with other ideas in order to control the air —the life.

P.E. What other ideas did you come up with?

PANITZ For instance, choosing an etude, taking a big breath and going to a certain point. If I could manage two measures, I would stop at that point. I would take another big breath and go for another two measures, and do the entire etude that way. I would go back and take the same dynamics and the same tempo and go for two measures and let's say, one more eighth. Then I would mark that throughout and go exactly the same amount, go back, and go for two measures and a quarter. All game playing, but it makes practice more interesting. I sometimes practice breathing while I am driving in the car.

P.E. How do you practice breathing in the car?

PANITZ I watch the mile markers on the road and I take a breath; I let it out slowly to see how long I can go. At sixty miles an hour, can I get a mile or a mile and a quarter?

P.E. How do you set the mood of a piece for yourself? The attitude?

PANITZ As a player, you can set the mood by visualizing a setting — let's take the piece *Syrinx*. On a dimly lit stage, you see Pan on a rock stretching and getting up. Then the excitement grows, as he starts to go through the forest and catches sight of his beloved and chases her. She avoids him. The excitement grows some more as she peeks around the trees and he chases her until she is changed into reeds. He plucks the reeds and makes the first of Pan's pipes. I feel that those last few notes in the piece could be his tears dropping into the water. The playing of these last few notes should be slightly air punctuated — instead of just legato — "Pluck, pluck, pluck." *Syrinx* has a number of clues for interpretation, but if a piece doesn't have many clues, then you have to use your imagination. That is really the difference between abstract music and programmatic music. When you play a sonata or a concerto, there is no other clue except tempo and dynamic markings, which you may or may not use. There you have to use a greater imagination. You should ask yourself, "What is the character of this theme? Is it bravado, tender, male or female, the mean papa or the understanding mama?

P.E. How do you show your students that music keeps going between the bar lines and notes?

PANITZ I simply say to my students to forget that the bar line exists. The bar line is just a means of reading music more readily. The Gregorian Chant has no bar lines but you still have to know how to read it.

P.E. How do you approach phrasing?

PANITZ Just as an actor or an orator uses his words with timing and accentuation. For example, Martin Luther King's speech "I Have A Dream" is a tremendous orchestration. One did not have to believe him, in fact, you could be the biggest bigot in the world, but if you were analyzing his speech for its dramatic content, you would have to say, "That was a masterful oration." He built it, everything flowed as it should, the intensity grew, he got more insistent, and he knew when to stop. A poor speaker's words do not flow. In music, just as in acting, the words have to flow to the right place. You have to know where the resolutions and relaxations are.

P.E. In fingerings, in slurring down from a C sharp to an E, you want a clean break. How do you work for this?

PANITZ A lot of lip. Follow the stream of sound. Follow the sound through, so that it is connected. This is done with the air and the embouchure.

P.E. How do you teach phrasing?

PANITZ I try to show my students that phrasing and articulation are a way to get to the meat of the music — it is not just expertise that enables you to slur or tongue x

number of notes. If I change articulation, it's to bring out a musical line. If you have a passage where you feel there is a scale line that needs bringing out, it's simpler to bring it out in two slurs and two tongues — "Deeataa-te-deeataa," because you could press the first note into a slur note. You could bring out that one voice. The flute is a very florid instrument, which plays a lot of notes, so you have to find the trees in the forest and not just the whole forest. The articulation does help you to bring out the skeleton line of what you have to say because you are playing with a lot of ornamentation. The flute is very ornamental, in contrast, let's say, to the tuba or the timpani. They may have one note in a measure and more often than not, you get the skeletal outline from them but we are the whole body. We've got all the skin, bones and animal fat on it and they have the skeleton.

P.E. Some players consider it impure to use fake fingerings or harmonic fingerings. Do you use them?

PANITZ Yes, it's knowledge. There are times when the ability to play one note with different fingerings can be a big help. If you are caught with a single note in your normal fingering and it's out of tune and you can't do very much with it, if you have alternate fingerings to move to, you have control. I teach many sympathetic fingerings. Knowledge is power. I just changed a fingering in a piece today—a high G trill. I fingered something differently and made the pitch better. Many times, I use fingerings that are not too common. I use them to make the pitch of a trill better than it normally is in the fingering charts. I don't consult anyone about it. I have just figured them out over the years. Maybe others have written them out and I am doing it the hard way but I have enough of them at my command.

P.E. How do you teach your students to shape a piece? Do you use certain pieces?

PANITZ I just try to make them happy with what they are playing. If they are interested, they could learn from anything. Most of the pupils know the basic rudiments of rhythm and fingerings. He could play the hardest piece in the repertoire only in one way and that is by being able to play it so slowly that he could manage it. One could play the hardest piece in the repertoire perfectly, if one could play it slowly enough. But then, there is a learning process involved there too. Because, although it would be so slow that it would be unbearable, yet, if it's perfect, that means all the relationships are the same and correct. Everything is relative, right? All the measures may be three yards long compared to later when they will be a quarter of an inch long. Just as you are related to your parents, you are still their daughter and you are five foot six now but you were still their daughter when you were one foot tall — the relationship is still the same, although the lengths have changed. I would like to show them things that could take them through all of music. Regardless of the differentiations I would make stylistically, interpretatively or from one proportion to another, I would like to show them things that would be usable down the line.

P.E. Do you do anything special to preserve intensity when you are playing pianissimo?

PANITZ I work very hard. Many players, it seems, who

try to play pianissimo, relax too much and I think that's wrong because then the sound doesn't go anywhere. It doesn't have the intensity. Whereas, if you support well, it will project.

P.E. I have read that you said, "Never try to predict projection." Could you tell me what you mean?

PANITZ I have found instrumentalists whose tone seems really big close by but when you walked away from them, the tone did not project as far, but the smaller tone that you heard next to you travelled farther. I don't know what the physical processes are but that is an observation on my part.

P.E. How do you know when you are projecting?

PANITZ Because I work and sweat. Sounds change depending on the hall. I know what I think I have to know to get the sound going out there; of course, the only real way you are going to know is when somebody comes down from the peanut gallery and says, "Gee, I heard you come through on the pianissimo." It's hard to predict your own sound because you are enveloped by it.

P.E. Do you have a way of making scales interesting to your students?

PANITZ It is not a question of interest but of impressing upon them that learning the scales is not just an exercise. I have them play the scales on seven different tonalities. It's like learning the dialects of a language. The scale on a tonic is the language and then when you play it on its seven different tonalities within the scale — each one sounds different. It is similar to modal scales. It gives you total control of the language itself and that is enough of a challenge.

P.E. What does it mean to you when someone says, "His sound cuts through the orchestra?"

PANITZ It has to do with the conductor who is doing the job. Some conductors don't like to cut down on the string section so you have to be able to play louder. It behooves the individual player to have as large a spectrum of dynamics as possible so that he can play with good control. There are times, when if you cut through, it's fine, but there are times when you have one hundred and six people against you playing fortissimo — you are not going to cut through. The flute is not a trumpet. The question is to get the right balance for the right piece and if possible, to play a solo pianissimo and give the right effect—if you could get the right balance of the orchestra to help you do that — I think it's beautiful. Otherwise, it would be too much of a piano or mezzo-forte or whatever it may be at the time. You can't judge one player's pianissimo against another's pianissimo. Many times you may see a part that comes from another conductor and it's marked one way or another and you play what you think the marking is from that man's orchestra and he says, "No, that is too loud." "Well, it's been marked up," you say. You have to be flexible.

P.E. Some players who perform with chamber groups regard playing in the orchestra as a *tutti* effort. What do you think about this attitude?

PANITZ Even if you play only one note that is held for five seconds, you have to try to make that a part of the musical experience. Instead of saying, "This is just a held note—no one will know what I do with it," you have to try to make it as interesting for yourself as part of the whole. I just don't sit back and blow tuttis and all of a sudden come on and play the solo. I feel that I am part of the whole and whatever I am doing in a tutti passage may have effect on the overall piece itself.

P.E. It seems to me that you are of quite an independent character.

PANITZ I try to maintain my own. When I joined the orchestra, the maestro called me in and asked, "Did you ever hear our recording of *Scheherazade*?" I had never played *Scheherazade* because I had never done much of the classics before joining the orchestra.

P.E. That's a surprise. How did you get the job?

PANITZ At Eastman the program wasn't geared towards the old masters but towards modern music. I felt more at home in that idiom than I did in the classical field.

P.E. What did you do when you began playing in the orchestra?

PANITZ I had to sight read a lot. In fact, my first three concerts with the orchestra were without preparation or rehearsal. The men were on strike and they had been given permission for some special concerts. One was a Uations memorial concert for Dag Hammerschold and on the program was Beethoven's *Ninth* which I had never played. I perspired a lot. As I do at all the concerts. When Ormandy called me in and asked me about the piece, I said, "No, I haven't played it." And then he asked, "Have you heard our recording of it?" and I said, "No." He said, "Well, I'll lend you our recording of it." I said, "As soon as we finish our recording of it, I'll listen to it. Thanks a lot." He was worried that I wouldn't know what to do and I was under the opinion that either I was going to be me and not an imitation of my predecessor—so I gambled on that and it worked out because I am still here after seventeen years.

P.E. You have toured extensively with the orchestra.

PANITZ Yes. Join the Philadelphia Orchestra and see the world.

P.E. You went to China and bought a Sheng flute.

PANITZ Yes. It's made out of seventeen bamboo pipes with one mouth piece and it's quite complicated. It's beautiful when the Chinese play it. I can play the regular Chinese flutes. A vegetable membrane covers the hole between the embouchure and the first fingering hole and it has a very exciting sound if you get the membrane just right. It can be too tight or too loose. There is a technique to it. When we recorded the *Yellow River Concerto* I played the Chinese flute. The membrane fell off in the midst and I tried to put another one on. I was not very expert at it. They use a glue which comes from a root. One wets the area around the hole and rubs the root on the bamboo. That makes the membrane stick.

P.E. How did the orchestra in Red China play the classics?

PANITZ Let us say they are not up to our standards yet. They rehearsed the second movement of Beethoven's *Fifth* and there was much to be desired. They don't have the best instruments. When they play their own music they know what they're doing. Those that I heard on the Chinese flutes were fantastic. Left handed and right handed. They play both ways. We were entertained once by the grand master of the Chinese flute. Much of the music sounded like foot tapping music and had a lot of charm. It was folk music.

P.E. How do you give your students special preparation for auditions or international contests?

PANITZ I try to get them to know the repertoire, of course. Today, most of the orchestras send out a list of the repertoire that they want you to play. It's not quite as blind as it used to be. It creates a greater sense of honesty — everybody knows they are going to have to play these particular pieces and a piece of their own choosing.

P.E. Why is it that at auditions and concerts — sometimes the best players don't do as well?

PANITZ It has to do with the personal psyche that is involved. Some people can knock off an audition as if it were nothing. Other people who are very fine players, get very tight. Yet, if they were sitting down in an orchestra they might be able to deliver the goods.

P.E. Again, it's being relaxed.

PANITZ Yes. I wasn't a very good audition player. I hated it. I am sure that most everybody does. However, it's the only way. You have to do it. I don't think that there is any secret. You have to be well prepared, know what you are doing and hope for the best. It is a question of luck, perserverance and preparation. Nowadays you have many auditions behind a screen. Orchestral committees and conductors choose. Some listen with one thing in mind and some may listen for something else. Generally, technique is what people listen for. A few weeks back in the New York Times, Rampal said that he plays fast because audiences like it. There is no answer to auditions except playing them and hoping that one day you will hit, hoping that that particular day everything is going for you. You can play all the notes but it doesn't necessarily mean you are saying something musically. I, personally, would be listening to more than technique because technique is an equalizer. Technique on the instrument is not all that difficult. I listen for imagination. We have to interpret. There is no one set interpretation. If there were, there would be no need for the different artists to play the same piece.

P.E. In intonation, is there an embouchure that is most difficult?

PANITZ Everybody's embouchure is different. Everybody blows their own way. My feelings on intonation are that nobody is right. I don't mean that the world is wrong and I am right, I mean, that you cannot say that because I am holding a note and I am sure that note is in tune, that makes it right. If the chord is out of tune, then it is out of tune and I must try to adjust my note to help. If the bottom of the chord starts to raise up and you hold on to the note, you are going to be blamed for the one who is wrong in the chord because high sounds penetrate. Intonation is being flexible and going where it may lead. If I let go of a note, let's say with the oboe and it's perfectly in tune and then he lets go, if I hang on, I may all of a sudden be out of tune. I was right when he was playing but if the oboe lets go and suddenly I realize I am left alone with somebody who is sharper than I am — then I have to do something. I can't stay there. You can't say, "I know I am right because we were right just a second ago."

P.E. Reality keeps changing. What do you think is the most a teacher can do for a student?

PANITZ To help them develop a concept. To let them understand it with their mentality so that they are not being led by the nose. You show them what you would do and then see if they can do it better. Don't just say, "Now this is the way to do it," because you have to have retention, and you have to be able to utilize your knowledge — not just for one piece but for other pieces as well. To develop a thinking mentality is more important than being able to imitate. There are not too many teachers who want to question to such a degree. "Why did you do such and such? Why did you breathe here?" I welcome that kind of observation — that investigation. Hopefully, if I have an answer I will give it to them honestly.

P.E. What is your definition of technique?

PANITZ To be able to play all the notes at whatever tempo you want to play them at, with a great clarity and a minimum of finger clicking noises. And that the sound be supported from one note to the next rather than any extraneous noise or key sounds that occur between notes. We play x number of notes to every note a brass or bassoon player plays. As the instrument gets smaller, it demands more technique. The potential has to be greater, the fingers have to move faster, and the tongue has to move faster. When I was at school, I couldn't learn how to double tongue. I knew I was a dead pitch, if I couldn't double tongue, so I had to invent something that would serve the purpose.

P.E. What did you invent?

PANITZ I don't want to say.

P.E. Really?

PANITZ It's just that I don't use any syllable in the throat. The normal syllable is in the front of the tongue and one in the throat. I went ahead and invented something which turned out to be better.

P.E. What did you do?

PANITZ I tell that to my pupils. I can't give it away.

P.E. But you wouldn't be giving it away — you would reach many other pupils.

PANITZ Let them come and ask me.

P.E. All right, I give up this time. Do you find that life prepares you for music or that music prepares you for life? Or is this too dramatic?

PANITZ I believe that life prepares you for music. For instance, from my background, when I went to college, I took sociology and psychology and various other courses that did not have any bearing directly on music. I think the broader an education you have the more you can apply to your music. If you are stuck in your own little cell of music, without knowing what is going on in the world, I don't think you can make music.

P.E. You seem to be a practical and simple man.

PANITZ I am practical and simple. I don't think you have to expound on something to say it. Musically, it is the same thing. You don't have to make all kinds of analytical statements. There are generalities that one could use throughout music and you try to encompass non-generalities with the particular style and you try to make certain differences. I don't try to play Bach the same way some people think Back should be played. If I have a better instrument than Bach, then I want to use it. I think that if he were alive today he would want to hear a modern day instrument — he wouldn't want to hear a baroque flute. I am not going to go to a Bach concert dressed in knickers, hose and in a carriage. I am going to arrive in a car and I am going to play Bach as he might have wished it to be played and according to the capabilities of the instrument and the players. I try to do it how he meant it to be and with my own imagination. In the notation that we have, not everything is written down. The inflection isn't there — it's the words. What makes Olivier greater than John Smith doing Hamlet? It's what he does with the imagination and what he does with what is there. I think the same thing applies to music. There are the notes but Bach did not write too much in, as far as articulation and dynamics, but that does not mean there wasn't any inflection at that time. Does that mean there was no emotion at that time? Does it mean there is no emotion in Bach? After all, he had twenty-one kids. Too often, when I hear Bach, it is dead. They are trying to duplicate what the old text says and it's like putting a sausage in a slicing machine and setting it on automatic and letting it slice out one slice after another. But this is a personal opinion and that's what makes show biz. I know there are people who think I am terribly wrong in the way that I play Bach but I don't really care. I am going to do it the way I think it sounds best and most interesting to myself and I think, to the audience.

P.E. Have you had your difficulties with conductors?

PANITZ NO! I feel that if a conductor leaves me alone in a certain passage, I will do it my way. If, on the other hand, thank goodness, it hasn't frequently happened, he wants something in particular — he has his own particular concept, I believe it is my duty to give him what he wants because he is the overall painter of the piece. I am just a cog in the machine but left to my own resources, I play it as I desire. I feel I have enough control over the instrument to do what anybody wants me to do.

P.E. I get the feeling that you're a good poker player.

PANITZ I used to play pretty well.

MARY LOUISE POOR

MARY LOUISE POOR

Mary Louise Poor received her Bachelor of Music degree from Illinois Wesleyan University, where she also taught flute, and her Master of Music from the University of Michigan. Her teachers have been Rex Elton Fair, Otto Krueger, John Wummer, Gaston Grunelle, Gaston Blanquard, Marcel Moyse and with Nadia Boulanger at the Conservatoire Americain in Fountainebleau, France.

Ms. Poor has taught on the elementary, high school and college levels, including positions at Murray State College, Ky.; Ball State University, Ind.; Mankato State, Mn.; Northern Illinois University, DeKalb, Ill. She has also served on the faculties of the National Music Camp, Interlochen, Mich. and the International Music Camp, Dunsieth, N.D.

Ms. Poor's teaching experience also includes that in Woodstoch School in the foothills of the Himalayas during her residence in India. She has performed as soloist in New Delhi; Bangkok, Thailand; and Kathmandu, Nepal. She has also been featured on radio broadcasts from Paris and Fontainebleau, France. Ms. Poor also writes and edits for Edu-Tainment Publishing Company, notable among her collection is "The Guide to Flute Teaching."

SETTING

Henry David Thoreau said, "The more things you can leave alone, the richer you are." But there are some things you cannot leave alone. Mary Louise Nigro Poor has picked up her career where she left it twenty-three years ago.

"I refused to play for nothing anymore. I was stuck up in a little country town in Minnesota with my babies — who I adore, but I didn't see anybody and I didn't hear anybody. Finally, I thought, I'm going to have my cake and eat it too — no matter how hard it is."

I met Mrs. Poor after a concert she gave at Carnegie Recital Hall. A handsome woman with a broad, kind face, wavy short brown hair and friendly eyes, she greeted me warmly and with great interest and encouragement for the book.

After speaking with admirers bringing flowers backstage, we went with friends and her accompanist, Max Yount, to the Carnegie Tavern for steins of beer and sandwiches. It was midnight, but Mrs. Poor talked on and ate heartily — "Playing takes a lot of energy."

The next day at 2 p.m. I met Mrs. Poor at the Barbizon Hotel for Women. We made ourselves comfortable in one of the sitting rooms decorated with white thirties furniture, flowered wallpaper and piped in Musak. We had just about an hour for the interview since her plane was leaving at 4 p.m. Dressed in a blue pantsuit, low heeled shoes and wearing a gold watch and earrings, Mrs. Poor sat, her hands on the table, calm and professional.

Her voice was warm and she spoke in a steady, purposeful rhythm, and listened carefully to the questions. Much in evidence, was her tremendous knowledge of art and music, life experience and her concern for her students. Her travels in India, Pakistan, Thailand, Sienna, Vienna and Salzburg have fired her natural curiosity in new music and music of other cultures.

An embracing person, she touches one with her compassion, givingness and courage — qualities which illuminate her music. She is finally rooting her musical and spiritual struggle in her life.

INTERVIEW

P.E. After your concert at Carnegie Recital Hall, you said you could not make a living playing recitals. What have the difficulties been for you in regard to playing recitals and gaining recognition?

POOR The difficulties have been being in the right place at the right time. The right place and time for me was about twenty-seven years ago — before flutists were as popular as they are now. I had to make a choice and who knows whether your choices are correct or not but I had to make a choice between accepting my scholarship at the Juilliard School or continuing my teaching at Ball State University in Indiana to help put my two younger sisters through school. I was twenty-three at the time. My father had started me on the flute when I was ten or eleven. Although Juilliard is a fabulous school and if you have the potential, it's more apt to be discovered there than anywhere else in the country, I felt that at that time, I should put aside my personal ambitions so as to allow my younger sisters to go to school. I had gone to the University of Michigan which was a good school but certainly not of the caliber of Juilliard. I began doing as much playing as I could do and after that, I went to Fountainebleu in order to study theory and composition with Madame Boulanger and then I went to Paris to do my study with Jacques Crunelle but a year or two afterwards I got married — that is where the separation point truly began. When I got married, twenty-five years ago, a woman was not as able to pursue her own career as she is today. I had been raised in the traditional manner that when a woman got married she stayed home and raised a family.

P.E. You believed in that?

POOR At the time, I did. *I no longer do.* It had such a drastic bearing on my own career. There was no way — once I started having my own family, that I could reverse this. I often speculate what if I had pursued it as seriously then as I am now — now that my family is grown and I am more free to do this. But I have to have a . . .

P.E. A stoic sense of humor?

POOR Yes, I have to have this kind of philosophy, otherwise, I can become very bitter because I feel I could have fulfilled my potential had I pursued my career full time at the age when I was most able to do it well.

P.E. Do you think you have less energy now?

POOR Physically the human body and brain are most able to learn things and to perform in your early twenties rather than in your forties. Everything that I do now, had I tried to do it some years ago, it would have been easier for me.

P.E. Do you think you could maintain the same stamina by eating right and exercising?

POOR Oh, yes. I am a great believer in health foods proper exercise and the proper kind of living. I'm a great vitamin taker. All of this makes a great difference in how I play today and how my body feels and how I will play ten or fifteen years from now. Our American diet is so bad that I try to do everything I possibly can to help this, because I feel we can prevent the degeneration process. I am working very hard to prevent this aging process from over taking me before I could accomplish what I want to. There is a certain amount of determination you have to have — "I know I could do this," instead of saying, "That is too hard."

P.E. Your turn of mind influences everything. Getting back to the question, if it's difficult for you to get recitals. . .

POOR Yes, it is. While I have quite a reputation as a teacher and a writer because I wrote for the *School Musician* for thirteen years there are many teachers who are great teachers but are not good performers. And so somehow or other. . .

P.E. You got typed?

POOR Yes, I think so. The problem is you could get hurt and you have to disprove some of this business, "Well, she is a teacher — she is not a performer." If you are lucky — if you are at the right place at the right time, you can get someone else to promote you. Here you are in the midwest; the promotion there is not what it is in New York. The other jumping off place is the music department in a large university or college.

P.E. Right now you are doing what you started to do when you were twenty-three.

POOR Yes, and there is an audience for it. The flute is a very popular instrument. Lots of youngsters are playing it. Since I returned in 1972, it's been just in the last four years that I've re-established my identity as a teacher and performer.

P.E. Once you returned, did you set up goals for yourself?

POOR Yes. The first thing I had to do was to again begin publishing. The second thing I had to do was to re-establish my contacts in the professional world.

P.E. Calling up people?

POOR Yes, flute companies, the colleges and universities in the midwest.

P.E. You handled all the correspondence?

POOR I was my own promoter. And now I have someone who takes care of the New York part of it. Again if you are lucky, like Paula Robison for example, and she is a fine flutist and fine musician but she was at the right place at the right time — Leonard Bernstein heard her play when she was about eighteen. Once you have that, it's just clear sailing from then on. She went to New York and she was always there.

P.E. How do you prepare for a recital in regard to practicing, choosing repertoire, physical and mental preparation?

POOR Taking those in order, as far as practicing is concerned, because I have a heavy teaching load of thirty and forty hours a week of private teaching and then I have a lot of driving time going between places — some of which I hope to eliminate, my practice time is very limited. Fortunately, I practiced very hard when I was in high school and college and I built myself a firm technical foundation. This is what I tell all of my high school students — you never know what's in store for you as far as your future is concerned, but if you practice hard now and build your technique — build a really strong foundation, you will be able to set your flute aside temporarily here and there when it's necessary and it will return to you because it's so strong and so secure to begin with. That is what happened to me; I had a good foundation when I was in high school. I studied with a very marvelous man, Rex Elton Faire, in Chicago. Mr. Faire wrote some method books. He was the teacher in my life and I have been to a lot of other people throughout the world.

P.E. What did he stress most to you?

POOR Basic technique. Scales, etudes — no long tones, partly because I didn't need to because I was blessed with a natural sound from the beginning. I had tried a number of other instruments when I was a child — my father was a band director.

P.E. What other instruments did you play?

POOR I played the cello. That was my minor instrument. I love the cello and I have a son who is going to be a fine cellist — I hope someday. Being able to play a lower string and having to concentrate on it for a number of years as my second instrument, has helped me because it allows me to hear things in a better perspective while playing in an orchestra. Thinking of the orchestra as an instrument and how it functions and the relationship of high to low.

P.E. Since you don't have much time to practice, have you worked out a warm up before a concert?

POOR I try to ration my time so that I spend a good ten minutes, and this is very small, of technical warm up. One of my first studies is octaves. I wrote a book called "The Guide To Flute Teaching" in which I outlined my analysis of how I play. I put in the terminology so that a band director would be able to read the book and say, "Okay, this is what I have to do to teach this youngster to play." In that, I had stressed the study of octaves and I used the octave slurs as a warm up. I have my own sheets that I give to my students and then some scales and chords which I try to spend a few minutes on. Then if I have a program or piece to prepare in a hurry, if it's a brand new piece, I go through it to find out where the technical difficulties are and then I make exercises of those. *I don't waste time playing from beginning to end. I simply go to where the problems are.* Then when I can get together with the pianist or the harpsichordist, we work out the ensemble, the phrasing and sometimes it takes a very long time to really get into a piece of music. It depends upon the style and the period of the music. My knowledge of art and literature also play a great, great role in my approach to the music itself. I have worked out a technique where I could learn things — so I never memorize anything because I have an insatiable curiosity about a great deal of music. There have been certain periods in my career where I have concentrated on one area and then another — I think most people do

this. I want to touch on many styles. I don't memorize easily and so I don't waste the time memorizing.

P.E. You realize your limitation?

POOR Absolutely! I think we all have to do this. You find out your limitations by experience. I finally decided that there was a great deal of emphasis put on memorizing that was unwarranted. I don't think that the fact that a person has a memory for remembering an entire piece is as important as how it's played. It's just like Rubenstein said in his book *My Young Years*, "I have inherited a photographic memory from my father who absolutely knew nothing about music," he says, "Being able to memorize has nothing to do with whether or not you are a musician, it is simply a trick of the mind. I have this. When I play, I turn the pages in my mind. It has nothing to do with whether I play the music well." I feel the same way. I cannot memorize very well so I prefer to spend my time learning new music, studying it in terms of its period, technical difficulties and the style in which I think the composer wanted it.

P.E. When making up a program, what do you have in mind?

POOR I make an effort to play a different program in order to set me apart from other people. It is very easy to find all Baroque programs or all modern programs and at either end of the spectrum, I think it's very easy for a certain amount of boredom to set in. Boredom not only on the part of the listener but I could sense a certain kind of boredom on the part of the performers. They may not think that it's there but I have the feeling sometimes when I hear this restrained approach to Baroque music or the way some people play Bach. I am bored as a listener.

P.E. What do you mean by a restrained approach to Baroque music? Are they almost afraid?

POOR Yes, afraid to apply any of the natural impulses that come from the sheer beauty of playing the gorgeous music, because they are afraid of being criticized. For example, the Bach that we played at Carnegie is one of the loveliest Bach pieces that I know of. It is a suite in C minor which was discovered in a sketch which was to be a suite for Lute — they think it was for lute. I am using the edition that Rampal and Veryon-Lacroix put together and they did a beautiful job and it's one of the most exciting pieces that I know of. I love it! I play it with all of the feeling that I have for the music. I don't think that Bach's music should be played coldly so I play it sometimes very romantically. I listen to recordings of the Bach sonatas but I never play the Bach sonatas in public for the simple reason that everyone else does. This is how I choose my programs, but first of all I consult with my keyboard player. I have alerted music publishers and stores that the minute they see anything contemporary for flute and harpsichord, without having to transcribe it in any way, something originally written for it, to please send it to me. We have read through stacks and stacks of music.

P.E. How much time do you devote to finding and choosing repertoire?

POOR Max Yount, my harpsichordist, and I try to get a pile of it and then we might spend two days of four or five hours each of just reading through the music and then putting it aside and going back to it, because sometimes the first reading is not fair. When we go back, we select things that we think deserve a second reading and a third reading. Sometimes things get better to us and more exciting and sometimes things get worse and we discard them. We also try to program it so we don't have all the old music at the beginning and all the new music at the end. Again, this keeps the audience more alert and it keeps us, the performers, more alert because of the different moods. It keeps things exciting. When I attend a concert, I don't want to hear something I hear on the radio all the time or what I could on my recordings — I want to hear something that will really get me excited. I want to say, "Wow, I'm really glad I went to that concert!"

P.E. I remember Samuel Baron saying, "A concert should change your life."

POOR Exactly. It should bring interest in the music to a lot of non musicians. Choosing the right kind of a program — like ending my concert with that little Donizetti which is a light, fluffy piece written by a composer who wrote this sonata when he was very young. You know, music is the only art in which you have to have a middle man. When you go to the Metropolitan Museum of Modern Art, you can see the artist's creation on the wall and it is just you and what he created but with music you have only a written page until you hear it. You need me as a middle man to re-create this music. It is a constant re-creation. This is why we can't say, "Well, this is right and this is wrong." We have to say, "Yes, I liked what he did or I didn't like what he did, but he has got the right to do it as long as there is a certain respect for the priod of do it as long as there is a certain respect for the period of were done in the Renaissance, Baroque and Classical period. You must have a certain respect for it without getting out of the bounds of good taste.

P.E. How do you define good taste in music?

POOR That's a difficult question to answer. Good taste is something that is not overdone or underdone. Good taste is something that will not offend.

P.E. You are not born with good taste — you acquire it. . . .

POOR Certain people are born with it perhaps but I think it has more to do with one's environment. When I was living in Salzburg I had a good friend who was my German tutor and she said, "You know the German word *kitsch*?" At that time I did not, so she said, "Well we are going to go shopping today and I'm going to show you what kitsch is." We went to tourist shops and looked at some very garish coffee table art. But some people do have a natural flair for elegance which their environment has helped them with.

P.E. Sometimes you are tempted to play a phrase differently or to give it more emphasis as you are crescendoing. . .

POOR Experience is a part of maturity and some

people do things more instinctively than others. Both my mother and father were musicians and so I inherited a certain amount of instinctive musicianship, but even so, when I go back and listen to my old recordings, I can hear how much I've changed. Maturity, in the light of my experience — not just my experience in playing music but my experience in becoming a mother and learning a great deal more about human relationships. My experience of travelling around the world twice and studying and experiencing different cultures. Hearing different kinds of music. I studied Indian music for a year and I played the sitar and the bamboo flute and an Indian came and sat on a floor and played folk songs — all of this synthesizes within a person.

P.E. You can't just play music — you are playing your life.

POOR Yes.

P.E. But you are also a lens through which the music passes. . .

POOR Yes, but your life experience — your ability to understand and to re-create this music is so directly influenced by your past experience.

P.E. How do you prepare physically for a concert?

POOR I try to get plenty of rest — seven or eight hours of sleep. But when I'm teaching and because of my hectic schedule, I go on six or seven hours, but then it shows up very strongly now particularly because I am no longer in my twenties. Through diet I always make sure I always have a great deal of protein and lots of fresh vegetables. I can't play on an empty stomach because I have to expend a great deal of energy. I am very athletic — I love to play tennis and ski. I have also learned to control the nerves up to a certain point. The more you play in front of people the easier that gets. I had a lung operation in 1968 and had half of my left lung removed. I did not play for about a year and it took me another year to begin to build up my physical strength. I worked very hard at it and I think I am even better at it now than I was before.

P.E. What did it take?

POOR Determination and practice — real determination.

P.E. Did you practice anything different or differently?

POOR The same scales and just gradually expanding it. *But I believe in the practice of yoga.* I don't do it a great deal but the philosophy behind it — the slow, careful breathing and movements. One of the most difficult times I performed was at flute convention in Milwaukee. There were three or four hundred flute players from all over the country. It's one thing to perform for an audience that doesn't know anything about the flute and another to perform for an audience in which they are all flute players. Some of whom are sympathetic and some of whom are not. Before I played, I just sat down and did slow breathing and said to myself, "I am not nervous." Mind over matter. I tried to sit there quietly and not think about the music — not think about certain passages that had given me certain problems. I just tried to be as peaceful and calm as I could — this was during the last five or ten minutes before walking on stage. This is a difficult thing to teach high school students. I have some fabulous students. I teach them more than how to play the flute. I have to teach them music. I have to teach them philosophy. I take it very seriously — it is a great responsibility to teach young people and I want to do everything I can.

P.E. Do you check out your instrument before giving a concert?

POOR When we work an instrument is just like an automobile; we have to give it regular maintenance. I went to the flute factory and spent a week there because I wanted to know more about adjustments myself. They were very kind to me.

P.E. Do you carry around a tool kit?

POOR I have a tool kit and I do on the spot adjustments for my students.

P.E. Can you order this tool kit or was it made up especially for you?

POOR Some of the men did make the tools especially for me but there is a company that sells other tools — so I have a complete tool kit now. Also, I always travel with a second flute.

P.E. At your recital, I saw an ivory flute and a bamboo flute.

POOR I have a variety a flutes. I have the alto, the bass, the piccolo and then I have a large collection of in between flutes before Boehm. I have the Baroque flute and a set of the plastic renaissance flutes and I have just acquired the conical, 1832 Boehm flute and that's the one I am not sure that I am going to continue to use.

P.E. How many recitals do you give a year?

POOR It varies from five or six to fifteen.

P.E. Have you unearthed any undiscovered flute pieces in libraries during your travels?

POOR No, I think this is for the musicologists and the scholars to discover. It is too time consuming.

P.E. What do you look for in a piece of music?

POOR The first thing I look for is that it be interesting.

P.E. What would make it interesting to you?

POOR Does it challenge me technically and if it does, is this a challenge that will be interesting to the listener. When I choose the music, I may want to play it for myself, but I can't program it unless I think it will be interesting for the listener.

P.E. Have you played electrified flute and tried playing micro-tones, whistle stops?

POOR Yes, I have tried this. When I left Pakistan in 1970, I went to Europe. My husband bought us a camper bus and I had four of my children with me, the fifth one was already in Europe, and we camped. Then I decided

to settle in Salzburg and then I went to Rouen, France for a week and then I decided to study in Vienna for the whole summer with Gazzelloni. I chose Gazzelloni because he was one of the first flutists who went to Darmstadt in Germany to work with composers.

P.E. He worked with Stockhausen, Boulez and Berio.

POOR Yes and he helped the composers by showing them what the techniques were for the flute. He is quite responsible for some of the wonderful things that have been published. I stayed in Europe for four years before returning to the United States and what was interesting to me was that most of the American style of avant garde music was with tapes rather than with only the instrument itself. But in Europe there are not many artists, who are established, such as Gazzelloni, who are willing to go to Darmstadt or the composer and get out on a limb and try these new things. Gazzelloni was willing to do this. This is something that Rampal has never been willing to do. He couldn't care less about that kind of music. He plays it maybe once or twice but many performers don't want to alienate their audiences by trying anything new — particularly in Europe.

P.E. They have to work harder against the old tradition — or try to incorporate the old with new.

POOR Yes. I was in Salzburg, Austria for two years and I bet I only heard one concert of contemporary music — there is more in Vienna than there is in Salzburg.

P.E. You aren't afraid of playing new music?

POOR On the contrary; because the competition is so strong in the traditional area, I feel I could make a little wave playing new music and also the most impelling reason is that my curiosity is so great about it. I have played Bach, Handel, Telemann and all the rest — my curiosity for new music is such that I have had to absolutely find out about it.

P.E. What have you found out about new music?

POOR I've found out that it's tremendously exciting and very challenging. But like anything else it can become very stereotype and boring. One has to choose very carefully. I did one of those pieces in New York.

P.E. Which piece did you do?

POOR *Rhymes for Gazzelloni* by Matsudaira the Japanese composer. The player has to have a bass drum, and a high hat cymbal and other things like finger cymbals and anything else that you would like to — it's very free. Gazzelloni used the echo chamber and I tried it two ways and I decided that the echo chamber was much more effective. You do some speaking and humming with the flute. I had to try this.

P.E. How do you practice for such a piece?

POOR You do practice it. You have to practice it but you never really know how it's going to sound until you get the amplification set up.

P.E. What flute pieces have been most challenging for you?

POOR The Romantic pieces, during the age of the virtuoso flutist, are all challenging. But some of the contemporary pieces are most difficult to do because it's very easy to fake it. Nobody else knows what they are supposed to be like and it's easy to say no one will know whether I am playing an F sharp or an F natural. One has to have the integrity to play what the composer has set there first, and then you could use your interpretation. I have found that these pieces are the most challenging technically.

P.E. How do you teach breathing?

POOR With the students who have had the most difficulty in breathing, I have tried to get them interested in yoga — the technique. It is relaxation. Much of the time, when they are playing their instrument — they're concerned about the sound, the fingering and then they are worrying about whether or not I am going to like what they are doing with the phrasing. I find that their breath is becoming shorter and smaller and they are getting tenser and tenser. So I say, "Hold it. Let's stop and relax and do the yoga technique of very slow deep breathing." Now you don't always have the time, when you are playing the flute or singing, to take a slow, deep breath — so then you have to learn the technique of being able to take a deep breath in a short amount of time. Bernard Goldberg is one of the few people who really gets down to the place that I am talking about. I never say to my students, "Breathe from the diaphragm." I say, "Breathe from the abdomen." It is also willing to use the entire torso from shoulder to pelvic area and relaxing all those muscles — to think of the lungs as being two balloons that have to be filled up. You have seen youngsters who take a breath and they will suck in the air and lift their shoulders. I say to them, "You can't get any air in your bones up there.

P.E. How do you teach a youngster about phrasing?

POOR The understanding of phrasing has to come from an understanding of basic music theory. And as I said earlier, I just don't teach my students to blow or how to finger the flute — I teach music along with it. I like to use material right from the beginning.

P.E. What kind of material do you like to use?

POOR Folk songs are very good. To find something that has a musical line that rises and falls so I could teach the children to breathe with the phrase is difficult but if they do this with folk songs — they can hear this.

P.E. The melody helps them to like what they are doing.

POOR Yes. And if it is a song, there are words there that are going to be helping them find the rise and fall of the phrase.

P.E. The emotional line. How would you define projection?

POOR The concept of tone that each person has. We often talk about a tone that is supported by the breath but this support doesn't mean a great deal unless the tone has a certain amount of tension. Tension that is going to carry through. I feel that the flute is the only wind instrument that is capable of the wide spectrum of tonal color, and I don't think a great many flutists explore this. Contemporary music allows us to be more free in the colors we use. I like to use this. I do try to use a variety of sounds. The projection, the variety of sound or the relaxation of the sound will be what is in my mind at the moment and what I want to do with that sound.

P.E. Do you think in colors?

POOR I do think in colors. I think of red, green and blue and of intensity. I think of relaxation. I am very, very interested in art. I surround myself with a variety of colors — from soft colors to strong colors — from intensities to pastels. I think of my sound in these terms and I think of texture — of hardness and softness.

P.E. Do you think of lines — cubes?

POOR Oh, yes. In modern music you have little spurts of sound that come out — like punctuation marks. With the flute, you can do so many things. I like to explore this. One of the reasons I like to play Twentieth Century music is that it offers more opportunity for exploration. There are certain formulas in earlier music which only allow you to go so far, and then you are beyond this good taste you were talking about earlier.

P.E. How do you teach different styles of music? Do you illustrate?

POOR Yes, I do and I try to get my young people to hear the different sounds on recordings and I try to get them to learn to identify various periods — Baroque, Classical, Romantic, Impressionist and so on. Then I choose certain works, for example, Handel sonatas in which I try to teach them basic theory and how to ornament in the stylistic practices of the time, the harmony and then for a student who has talent and I know is going to continue with their music, I try to choose all along at different levels music that is going to expose them to different periods within that level. In other words, Classical, Romantic and then a Baroque sonata — constantly going through all different periods of music so they will learn how we must vary our style.

P.E. And vary their programs — once they start giving concerts. Is there a difference in teaching methods with a student who wants to play in a band and one who doesn't?

POOR No there is not because the only difference is that of literature.

P.E. Have you ever worked with someone who had a disability? Someone who had braces or had lost a finger?

POOR One of my first experiences was with a spastic child who had a birth injury of the right hand — it was very poorly co-ordinated. The first instrument that they had put her on was the french horn so her right hand didn't have to be used. Someone came along and said, "We're not doing this child a favor. Let's see if she could use the fingers of the right hand." They gave her a flute and I got her shortly after she had played maybe a year or six months. This child was determined to play the flute — she loved it. It took a great deal of patience and persistance on her part and it was a marvelous feeling for me, because here I was helping this child to realize a wonderful feeling of being able to create music with her disability. I also had a child who was hit by an automobile and had brain damage and I was able to help him a little.

P.E. Did you devise certain exercises for them?

POOR Yes, for this one girl I did devise certain exercises so she could develop the fingers of her right hand. Now, braces are a common problem. If the student has the ability to produce a good tone without braces, then that ability will not be entirely lost with the braces. It is simply a matter of having more stuff inside the mouth. They have to learn to compensate for that—which they do and then they have to learn to compensate for when the braces are removed. I never have had any great problem, but if I do have a student who comes to me with a severe inabilty to produce the right shape and this is a rarity—and I am unable to figure out a way or the student is unable to control the movements of the muscles to do what needs to be done to produce the sound in the flute—then I must be very frank and say, "I think you must try another instrument." That's very rare though.

P.E. How do you prepare a student for independent study? How do you help them understand that it is for a lifetime?

POOR We have to do this in the junior and high school stage where they are studying. I make sure that at every lesson we cover different types of material. We have scales, technical studies, we have our etudes and pieces and I don't vary from that very often except when we are getting ready for recitals and I have my students give recitals very early—junior and senior high schools or we might have contests—then we will have two or three lessons where we just concentrate on a piece. I always emphasize that they have to learn to divide their time according to how much time they have to practice and they must touch on everything and they must do it all the time. If they could only take their flute out for five or ten minutes, when they are really busy—college students who have courses—to prepare, and to try to do this.

P.E. Do you play just what is written in Classical music?

POOR Oh, no. In Baroque music the performer is expected to ornament it and so I do this. In the Romance, the *Sonata In D Major, No. 7*, I played a lot of ornamentation that was not written there.

P.E. How do you make your choice of ornamentation?

POOR A lot of repetition. I try different things and Max and I try different things together. We ask each other's opinion on it. But I am not going to change the notes that are written there—not unless we are going to play a French style where they wrote one rhythmic pattern but expected you to play another. That is the only way I would make any changes. I wouldn't change the basic music. I would only add the ornamentation that was expected of the performer at that time.

P.E. You do many flute clinics. What have you found

that students need to know most?

POOR It depends on where I go but a lot of them need to know how to take care of an instrument. Secondly, if they haven't had a flute player around because their band director is a brass player or it's a small area, they will come up to me with questions such as "How do you get such a big, low sound?" Well, then they need a basic embouchure and I give them my concept of how to get an even sound — the embouchure changes for each sound and each register because of the shape of the hole and the direction of the air. We have no octave keys so we have to talk about how to play in tune. They will also come up and say, "I played my B flat and it's in tune with that machine," (an oscilloscope). Then they will proceed to play out of tune. I spend a lot of time teaching them to learn about their instrument and how they play — a lot of it is sheer technical material.

P.E. What are the most difficult problems people have with the embouchure?

POOR One of them is making lip holes small enough. Very often, when they go into the low register they allow the lips to open more. In order to get the biggest sound in the lower register you need to make a smaller hole and get the direction right. You need to check the instrument because most of them leak. The extreme high notes are a problem because they will pinch and squeeze and get too tight. You have to teach them this flexibility and a basic understanding of the acoustics of the instrument — knowing that this is the only wind instrument in which not all the air which you are blowing is going into the flute. It's going here and there — how much goes here depends upon whether you are playing low or high. If you are playing low, more is going to go down and if you are playing high, more is going to go up. Also, some of them cover it too much and roll it back in and the shape of their lip effects it.

P.E. You have had to make choices between your family and career. Do you still find it difficult to pursue your career now that your family is grown? Do you find it more difficult for a woman?

POOR I think so partly because of my lack of opportunity up to this point but also because men feel very threatened by a woman who has enough aggressiveness to want to go out and compete with them. They won't admit it but I think it's true.

P.E. How do you detect it?

POOR Subtle put-downs. Maybe you don't get the job but the man does and you know very well that you are as good as he is.

P.E. What do you do then?

POOR I try to make myself better because I can't use that as an excuse. I can't say, "I didn't get this because I am a woman." I have to be sure in my own mind that I didn't get it because I wasn't as good.

P.E. What about satisfaction?

POOR I get a wonderful satisfaction from seeing a student grow under my guidance just as I have had the satisfaction from seeing my children grow. I have had students who have come back to me over the years and that is a marvellous feeling. It makes me feel that I have done some things right.

P.E. Now what do you do want to do?

POOR I want to play and go out and give more clinics and more master classes. But I don't feel a person has the right to be my kind of teacher without the ability to perform. I perform, therefore I have the right to teach.

P.E. Once you are able to teach what you do—you are mastering it.

POOR Right. I can't say, "I heard so and so do it this way—so this is the way you better do it."

P.E. When I spoke with Doriot Dwyer, I said, "You are in a man's world." She said, "I have always been in a man's world. I just didn't happen to join the Boston Symphony—I worked for it."

POOR She is very good. She started earlier. I remember when she got that job with the Boston symphony and I had just had my first child. I had known her when I was in high school—not very personally but she and I had competed in the contest together in Illinois when we were both in high school. I followed her career and she is a beautiful player but she had this concentration and she did work hard and got where she was going to go. It is a man's world and I just didn't get into it fast enough to compete on their level. A woman's role today is different compared to what it was twenty-five years ago, where the woman stayed at home and it was nice if she took in four or five piano students and if she played for the church.

P.E. What would you say to a young woman?

POOR I think she better look long and hard at what her goals are. I am not sure that being in the professional world with the terrific competition and the frustrations are going to be compensated for in a moment of glory. I have many moments of glory with my children and my family and the love and happiness I have found there and the music which is very much part of our lives has compensated for being famous—in a sense. Yet I still have the desire to want to play for people because I can make them happy with what I play.

HENRY ZLOTNIK

HENRY ZLOTNIK

Henry Zlotnik was born in Russia, a subject of Czar Nicholas II, on March 9, 1903. "I'm a Pisces, very fishy." He immigrated to America in 1914 with his sister to join his father, and settled in Hartford, Connecticut.

At twelve, he began studying the flute and by nineteen was the city's most active and popular player. He had his own radio show, played in the Hartford City Orchestra, taught the flute and on occasion, played supper music at Mark Twain's home. Upon hearing a recording of Georges Barrère, he felt he had to study with him, so he left for New York and enrolled at the Damrosch Institute of Music, now known as the Julliard School of Music.

In New York, he performed in almost every musical medium of the time: vaudeville, burlesque, silent movie theatres and broadway shows. On radio he played in the NBC, WOR and CBS orchestras. For many years, he performed in the Bell Telephone Hour Orchestra with such conductors as Sir Thomas Beecham, accompanying Jashua Heifetz and other great artists. He played in many of the legendary movie houses of the twenties and thirties — the Rialto, the Rivoli, the Capitol, the Roxy, the Strand and Radio City Music Hall. A highlight of his career was touring with Sousa's Band from 1928 to 1931 throughout the United States, Mexico and Canada.

He has been teaching in New York City since 1936 and today is recognized as one of the foremost teachers of the flute.

SETTING

Though quite a contemporary man at seventy, Mr. Zlotnik still has the old veteran about him — the Sousa Band trouper with sideburns and silvered moustache. Sportily dressed in a tweed jacket, navy blue trousers, light blue shirt and a red tie, he stood tall, his blue eyes crinkling, peering closely into my face, and while approachable and friendly, he has a way of sizing you up — usually while removing his spectacles, at once looking owlish.

His resonant voice boomed, often when playing the raconteur, a role he imperiously commands with his flair for the dramatic gesture, suspenseful weavings, impersonations and musician's brogue. He was startling but always amusing. His favorite is the morality tale, underscoring his need to teach — practically and thoroughly.

His studio is in an old building on Broadway filled with booking agents, singers, rehearsal rooms with mirrors and mellow sounding pianos. We sat by the window of his studio overlookng the audition route for New York City's actors, singers and dancers carrying their portfolios and satchels and never did the incessant hum and burp of city traffic leave us.

Stacks and stacks of sheet music, some yellowed at the edges, were placed in neat piles on tables about the room which was furnished with filing cabinets, a desk with papers and a big white clock on it, music stands, an antique mahogany music stand and in a corner was a glass bookcase filled with dark rows of books. On the walls, protraits of distinguished looking gentlemen, flutists of the past, with huge droopy moustaches gazed down upon us. The bright October sun warmed us and Mr. Zlotnik leaned back in a chair puffing on his pipe.

INTERVIEW

P.E. May we start off on a nostalgic note?

ZLOTNIK Well, what would you like to have me tell you?

P.E. I'd like to know the story behind the poster "The Spirit of 1776" in which you played the piccolo.

ZLOTNIK Oh, the poster was a still from a short I made. That goes back to 1927 . . . a little while ago. It was one of the first jobs I had. I didn't even play the flute, I played the fife. Anyway, this was the time when the talking pictures first began to come in and they wanted to make a short about the Fourth of July. For an audition, I had to play "Yankee Doodle." Then we went on location to do the battle scene. The drummer fell down and I walked around with a bandage on my head. For that I made one hundred and fifty-seven dollars and that's more than I ever made playing flute. It was a lot of money then. At the time, I was still a student at the Damorsch Institute of Musical Art named after Frank Damrosch whose brother was the conductor Walter Damrosch—anyway, now it is known as the Juilliard School of Music. Juilliard took it over because it had the money so then it became a larger outfit, but before, it had been very small with a student body of about 250 or 270. And by the time you were there two years, you knew everybody—students, teachers . . . it was a very intimate affair. We were real colleagues then. We tried to help each other out in every way rather than running everybody down in trying to get ahead. Well, coming back to the poster . . . it was really a still from a short which was shown in the movie houses for nearly twenty years afterwards . . . so, when you think about how much I got paid . . .

P.E. You were never paid royalties?

ZLOTNIK Oh no. I got paid once and that's all.

P.E. What was the minimum scale then?

ZLOTNIK It varied with each town. Let's see . . . the theatre scale was about seventy dollars a week working seven days and seven nights.

P.E. How many hours did you have to work?

ZLOTNIK As many hours as they wanted. In the theatre, you worked generally from noon to eleven or midnight—depending, with a two and a half hour break around five o'clock.

P.E. Were you paid for overtime?

ZLOTNIK Sometimes. And there were no days off—if you wanted a day off, you had to ask the contractor to let you have a substitute, which either he or you got, and you paid the substitute out of your own pocket when you got your salary. When the Union did get organized though, we finally got a six day week in the legitimate theatre but not in the movie houses. Don't forget that, in those days, between 52nd and 42nd Streets, there were ninety-one flute jobs available in the theatres.

P.E. Did you have to work less hours than in the theatre?

ZLOTNIK Yes, if you were employed as a regular houseman. Then you were paid a regular salary—so many hours and days per week. But most of the programs had individual orchestras and you were hired by the sponsor.

P.E. Would you tell me more about your radio experience?

ZLOTNIK Well, you had one shot at it, period. You were on live, and if you screwed up—that was it. Since time was money, they wanted to cut rehearsal time to a minimum. So they wanted musicians who could get together a half hour program in an hour and a half rehearsal. For many years, I worked on The Bell Telephone Hour. It was only a half hour program, but they required four hours rehearsal for it—they could afford it and Don Voorhees was independent enough. When big stars like Heifetz came, he would rehearse us six hours until perfect. Perfection in any of the arts is only enough rehearsing and practicing. No matter how good you are, you've got to rehearse. With Heifetz, he used to be as hard on us as he was with himself. He was concerned with the details. Also, I played with the NBC orchestra but not on a regular basis and on WOR, which had a large orchestra and the CBS orchestra too.

P.E. What did you enjoy about playing in these radio orchestras?

ZLOTNIK When you play under a good conductor, it is a great emotional satisfaction, but unfortunately in those days you travelled around from theatre to theatre and you played with lousy conductors—that was very frustrating and you couldn't speak your mind either—if you wanted to keep your job. Then, the performer was supposed to be an automaton, carrying out the conductor's wishes. Anyway, it's the conductor who is held responsible and blamed for a bad performance, not the player. However, when the relationship is right, like when I played with Sir Thomas Beecham, who was a marvelous and great character, not the greatest as far as baton technique was concerned, but his music sounded marvelous—know why? He let you play. As long as what you played fitted in, but not if you came in showing off.

P.E. I understand that you played for vaudeville acts?

ZLOTNIK Sure did! In the Palace Theatre. Oh, there were dozens of theatres. Some were vaudeville and moviehouses and others strictly vaudeville. The great years were the twenties and early thirties. But past the middle thirties marked the end for vaudeville and the talkies took over. To play in vaudeville you had to be a very good sight reader. They would pass the books for one act and while you were rehearsing that, they'd pass the books for another act. Also, you had to make good guesses, because many times there were red pencil marks crossing out things all over the books. For instance, you read "Cut" here and there, and then in green pencil "Don't cut." So you developed a sixth sense after awhile. Now this training is good for a certain type of musician. With experience like this, you could walk into an opera house and get a job.

P.E. How many theatres were there?

ZLOTNIK A tremendous amount. Most of them gone now, but there was the Capitol that had a hundred peice orchestra, the Rialto, the Rivoli, the Roxy which also had a large orchestra, the Strand ... none of them are here, they have all been knocked down but there were easily thirty movie houses then.

P.E. What happened to these orchestras when the talkies came in?

ZLOTNIK It finished the era. A lot of the moviehouse orchestras were cut out. So it didn't look so hot. It was 1928—before the crash and there were many signs. By chance, I was offered a job playing in Sousa's Band and I figured I better take it.

P.E. How did you get the offer?

ZLOTNIK The only way you got a job in those days was through personal contacts and demand. Two of my friends who were in Sousa's Band called me at the last minute because, when they were just about to start out, one of the fellows got sick. So the contractor, the personnel manager, asked around and my friends said, "Hey, we know somebody." So I got the call, and I went over and talked with the contractor. I'd be away twenty-four weeks playing fourteen concerts a week ... seven matinees and seven evening performances. That's pretty heavy.

P.E. You always played the same program?

ZLOTNIK Well, when you travelled around you had a matinee and evening program. That's all you needed because you were always in a different town but when you played location, I mean when you played anywhere for two or three weeks, like when we played the Steel Pier in Atlantic City, the Willow Grove in Philadelphia, we played a different program every night and afternoon. You never knew what would be in the books because you didn't rehearse. You had to play everything by sight.

P.E. How much did you rehearse before the tour?

ZLOTNIK Oh, you rehearsed a few days, but you rehearsed the standard program—the repertoire you were supposed to know. You see, the band was made up of players from all over the country and we'd meet in New York a few days before the tour. Sousa was a smart businessman. He wanted to arrive in any section of the country with some local person from the vicinity there. He had a tremendous following—packing them in solid. When I joined the band, Sousa was already seventy years old and a man of considerable means. He didn't have to travel around on trains everywhere. He was a remarkable man who took great care to find work for those in his band, whether he made money or not. Of course, he didn't have to worry, he left seven million dollars when he died. You know, to play in Sousa's Band, you not only had to be a very competent player, you had to get along with people—all those weeks on the road, sharing hotel rooms and bills —well, you had to be a pretty congenial fellow! Also, very neat—your uniform had to be clean and everything in place. He never tried to tell you what to do, but he never wanted anyone bringing any disgrace to the band. I look back very fondly upon the band. I was able to travel and see every state in the Union. I saw Canada, some Mexican towns like Juarez, Tiajuana ...

there's a Sousa Band Fraternal Society which meets on Sousa's birthday—November 6th, but there are not too many of us left, you know?

P.E. How many players were there in the band?

ZLOTNIK Seventy-six players.

P.E. What was the repertoire like? Did you play mostly marches?

ZLOTNIK No, we played marches as encores. The rest was old transcriptions and original things. We played Richard Strauss's *Don Juan*, overtures by Rossini, contemporary and some show music. At that time, the jazz bands were beginning, but he held his own with the older generation. He did have a saxophone and some jazz was played; but he was the last of the concert band era of the early 1900's.

P.E. How many seasons were you with Sousa?

ZLOTNIK Four.

P.E. When the crash came in '29, what did you do?

ZLOTNIK I got married!

P.E. What a celebration!

ZLOTNIK I still remained with Sousa although the trips got shorter. I'd be away about twelve weeks. He kept us working right up until he died in 1931. Then the band folded—it was very tied up with his personality.

P.E. Did you turn to theatre jobs then?

ZLOTNIK Oh, no, all along I worked in the theatres. You see, when I had to be away, I'd get a substitute so that when I came back, I'd have a spot. I played the Loews theatre circuit. They had something like sixty theatres in greater New York but again, when the talkies came, they cut out most of the neighborhood theatres' orchestras. They were pretty lousy anyway.

P.E. What was it like to play for silent movies?

ZLOTNIK You had a book filed with all loose music and you had to be prepared to play eight measures of this for a part and then go on to the next thing. You also had music for scenes and if you had six characters in the picture, you had six parts to play for each one or for each dramatic mood. There was all kinds of mood music. Usually the general music director would see the picture first and score music for it, not original music though. Now in the more independent and smaller theatres, the conductor had to go a few mornings and see the picture and then go to the theatre's music library, which was only available to him, and choose the music. The music chosen was a little bit of everything.

P.E. Television similarly avails itself to that. Hearing Beethoven's *Fifth* as background music for a toothpaste commercial—I sit there and get cavities.

ZLOTNIK Yes ...

P.E. Anyway, you had to be a very good sight reader, didn't you?

ZLOTNIK Oh, yes! Otherwise you couldn't get a job. I did a lot of substitute work and usually you didn't know what you'd have to play. So you had to be a good reader, and if you were, you were very much in demand—otherwise, you weren't hired.

P.E. Were there moments when you got lost in the score—with all those parts going on?

ZLOTNIK Then you learned to fake it enough to get by. This kind of training doesn't exist today.

P.E. But what about the quality of the playing?

ZLOTNIK The quality of the playing was not that good because the most important thing was to play the right notes . . . the correct notes. It wasn't fine and rehearsed playing. I considered it botch work.

P.E. What is the value of this kind of training?

ZLOTNIK Oh, you could walk into any radio studio orchestra and get work. Radio began coming in about 1925–1926; and there was lots of work and they paid you by the hour.

P.E. How much did radio pay then?

ZLOTNIK Ninety dollars a week. That was big money then.

P.E. What skills are needed to be able to play in an opera house orchestra?

ZLOTNIK Well, you must know the opera repertoire, and as I said, be a good sight reader and be able to make the right guesses. The Met, for many years, every time there was a vacancy, would send to Italy for a musician because no one in America had the experience to play opera; but this changed thirty years ago.

P.E. Maybe there were lots of Italians in the Met then.

ZLOTNIK Maybe! You see, in Italy there are opera companies at levels a, b, c, d, down to z. Those companies travel around from town to town. This way you learn a repertoire and when you're ready, you join a big opera house.

P.E. Weren't there other opera houses besides the Met at that time?

ZLOTNIK There was the Chicago Company and the Metropolitan—period. And really, there was only the Met because the Chicago Company only ran half season. So where was a player going to learn the repertoire? Where was he going to get the training? The conductor for an opera is very busy. He's got the soprano to worry about—not the third flute, so the third flute better know when he comes in because he's not going to be indicated.

P.E. You grew up in Hartford . . .

ZLOTNIK Yes, that's where I grew up and at nineteen I was already at the top of the heap there. I played in a twenty-five piece orchestra, I had a radio program I used to do on Sundays and I had a half a dozen students. So, I said to myself, "Where am I going? What good is it being a big shot in Hartford? Can I go to New York where the competition is keen and carve a notch for myself?" My friends thought I was crazy to give up all I had going. Anyway, I came here, entered the Damrosch Institute and got a job in a Staten Island moviehouse. I had to com-

mute from Staten Island to 122nd Street and West End Avenue everyday to attend the Institute. But all this stood me in good stead because by studying a few years, by the time things got tough, I had made a little notch for myself, so when the Depression came, I was able to remain in the music business while my friends back home, who were musicians, got out of music and never got back in.

P.E. Can you describe a typical lession with Georges Barrère?

ZLOTNIK Well, you learned mostly by imitation, I mean, by ear—by hearing him play. Most of the French teachers are like this. If you asked Barrère how he did something he'd say, "I cannot do for you, you make sound like this," or, "I don't know how I do, I do like this" and he would demonstrate. So you went home and cracked your brain to figure out how to get a sound like "this." I don't think much of imitation at all, but hearing Barrère in itself meant very much. He was a master. For me, he was the greatest flute player I ever heard. He impressed you that he had a more beautiful tone than he actually had, that he could tongue faster than he actually could, and that the flute had a greater dynamic range than it actually had. Barrère never played just on one line, on a monotonous line. For instance, everything is relative. If you want a passage to sound particularly beautiful, you play coarsely just before it—a little rough. Rampal is the nearest one who gives you a little idea of this and who does similar things.

P.E. It's lines of contrasts?

ZLOTNIK That's right. Contrasts all the time. If you want to play faster, you play the movement before it slower. So now the section sounds faster and actually is.

P.E. You're talking about creating the illusion?

ZLOTNIK But there's nothing wrong with that! This is art. Barrère used to drum into us, "Don't give it away. Don't give it away. Always have an element of surprise and contrast." The ear tires of the same thing. At the same time Barrère was around, there was this marvelous flute player in the Boston Symphony, before Doriot Anthony Dwyer, named Georges Laurent. He was a great flute player—he sounded wonderful in the orchestra, but in recitals . . . well, he played perfectly, everything was nice and smooth—but it was not exciting. With Barrère, on the other hand, he said, "Always leave them wanting more. Build up to a climax and stop."

P.E. How old were you when you began learning the flute?

ZLOTNIK I heard the flute for the first time when I was ten, but it wasn't until I was eleven or twelve that I began to save up money to buy a flute. And I was about thirteen when I began to study. I bought an old system flute with six holes and eight keys on it. It cost me twenty-one dollars and fifty cents. I had a newspaper route from which I made two dollars a week and from this I paid off the flute over a period of time. Three years later I had enough money to buy a Boehm flute.

P.E. With whom did you study in Hartford?

ZLOTNIK A very nice old German schoolmaster.

Herman Siewert was his name. He was a drill master, though; if you made a mistake, you had to go to the beginning and start all over again. So you could spend six weeks on it until you got it right. That sort of drill was good for me, but not on a regular basis . . . but it did give me a discipline. With Barrère, it was the reverse because you studied the piece and you worked to get the most out of it. Let's say, you've only gotten fifty percent out of it; well, that's it, and move on. Then you come back to the beginning, but only after you've gone through the entire piece. So, you put in another week and you get your one hundred percent. But if you put in another week in the beginning, all you get is another week of frustration. But old Siewert was a great encouragement to me; he advised me to go and study with Barrère. "Go and find out," he said.

P.E. When did you begin teaching?

ZLOTNIK Oh, back in 1936. I opened up a little studio next to a music store, which I rented for ten dollars a month. And I started off with a couple of students and gradually I built up. Also, since it was mid-town, I did a lot of playing at Radio City Music Hall. There, I did substitute work. So, in between, I could always come in and give a lesson.

P.E. What does teaching mean to you?

ZLOTNIK Well, if teaching merely consisted of calling out the wrong notes, that would be pretty boring. But if teaching means you can make a project out of each student, developing, aiming towards a goal, finding the answers through new avenues and old, then it's pretty rewarding for both of us. And as I tell the students, "I don't know all the answers, but I know a lot of them." And if I don't know, let's find out. I want them to find out what took place and not go entirely by feel and intuition . . . Well, I wouldn't say you can't go by intuition, but what I would say is that I've had students who intuitively, when they started playing, got into the right mood and feeling because they felt the music. Of course, I think this is the most marvelous way in which you can play music, but there is music which must be understood — like cerebral and constructed music. If you don't understand it, you can't play it. Bach's music is very structured and using just your intuition in music like that can lead you astray. Intuition is wonderful. It's part of a person's talent and nothing is better than talent. Nothing takes the place of talent.

P.E. What do you demand most from your students?

ZLOTNIK That they don't expect me to do their practicing for them or have a simple answer to all problems. It's intelligent practice that will eventually solve their problems. When they come to a lesson, they should be free to work on the music.

P.E. What is the best age for a youngster to begin to learn the flute?

ZLOTNIK Learning to play the flute at a too early age, let's say seven or eight, can result in bad habits, because the fingers aren't developed enough yet. I did have a student who I started off at seven because he was so very anxious to play. He would come with his recorder and ask, "Are my fingers big enough now?" Well, today he still holds the flute as he did when he was a child. You can't change it now. I believe a good age to begin is about ten or so.

P.E. What do you try to impress most on your students?

ZLOTNIK That if something is worthwhile achieving, it's worthwhile working for. Wishing for it will not achieve it. Unfortunately, as you know, some people can do it with a lot less effort than others.

P.E. Do gifted students tend to be lazy?

ZLOTNIK Generally speaking, the gifted student works the hardest. I did have one experience with a gifted student who wouldn't work, compared to a student with very limited talent who worked very hard and therefore, surpassed the other in the long run . . . after a good many years. He reached a level where his basic talent increased by acquiring the ability to do more.

P.E. Besides talent, what are the physical qualifications needed to be considered?

ZLOTNIK You can't have a very bad receding jaw or a very bad protruding jaw. Now, almost anyone can learn to play the flute and although it may take someone with a malformation a little longer has very little to do with later development. For instance, some of the finest players have mouths that are anything but symmetrical.

P.E. What about chest development?

ZLOTNIK As far as chest development, that's relative. It takes comparatively a small amount of air to play the flute, providing you can direct the air column in the proper place without wasting it. However, I would add that diaphragm control is as important to the flute player as to a singer.

P.E. And having a good ear?

ZLOTNIK The ear is an absolute necessity. If the ear is bad, the person will never play in tune, because the flute is not in tune to begin with. It has to be played in tune. The ear is necessary for all string and wind instruments but not so important for pre-tuned instruments like the piano or organ. Also, you can't teach aesthetics, musical taste and feeling — I mean, the realm of abstract things.

P.E. But you can guide a student, can't you?

ZLOTNIK Yes, guide and develop it, if it's there in the incipient stage. But if the person has no musical taste and everything has to be marked crescendo, diminuendo, staccato, legato, what will come out is a big square performance. The person must feel the music.

P.E. Can you define musical good taste?

ZLOTNIK That's difficult. It's dependent on the culture and the particular person. So, talking within the realm of this particular culture and what we consider good taste, maybe playing a phrase with expression but not too much so. What does that mean? It means nothing. You cannot gauge it precisely. Taste is what the person has digested, heard, acquired over the years, what he feels and likes. And if he hasn't been impressed by any of this, you have a performer without salt and pepper.

P.E. Do you think a child should learn another instrument before learning to play the flute?

ZLOTNIK Oh, yes! It will prepare them. You see, children have little tolerance as far as practice is concerned. They want to play music right away. So you certainly have to work with them very closely. Some children can be swindled into doing quite a bit of practicing, which gives them control of the instrument at the age when they can practice four times as much as they'll do it ten years later—when they'll want to do it. So they acquire a technique and by the time they are old enough to want to play, they have all this equipment. I did this with a few students, but this is a case where you have to know the child. One youngster (he's eleven or twelve), well I'm swindling him into doing a certain amount of technical things. He does them because I proved to him that if he does these things, it will go a little easier. So he believes me and he could see the end in itself. A child objects to practicing if he can't see what it's for—this applies to anybody.

P.E. Do you speak of music history, composers' lives, to a child?

ZLOTNIK Yes, this is very important for the child to get to know, but not in a disconnected way. It must correspond to what he's doing: then, you will reach him. Otherwise the handing out of historical information goes in one ear and out the other.

P.E. What do you think of the school's role in music education?

ZLOTNIK Don't get me started on that! What goes on in the schools is an abomination. Music should play a more important role in the schools and they should have very well trained people in order to reach the children. Today they don't even teach you how to read music. Did you know that an all-high school chorus in one of our larger cities sings by rote? They can't read music!

P.E. Is using literature instead of etudes for study a good idea?

ZLOTNIK No ... I object to taking a good piece of music and hacking it to pieces before you have the technique and ability to play it. By the time you learn it, it's creeping out of your ears and you hate it and you'll never play it again. Now, an etude can be used to study the particular technical problems of a certain piece, so when you get to the piece there is a feeling of accomplishment. If you hate the etudes, fine—who cares? That's not the point. But there are some etudes that are excellent in themselves and will be beneficial at all levels in your study. The Andersen Etudes are remarkable. Many of them can almost be played as concert pieces. They are worthwhile studying beyond the point of being a student.

P.E. Can you describe a typical lesson you might give to a beginner and an intermediate student?

ZLOTNIK With the beginner, it's setting up the standards and the priorities. Now, what is more important? To learn to hold it, how to blow it or to learn to finger it? After many years of teaching, you discover that the most important thing is to teach the student how to hold it. Because if he doesn't learn to hold it properly from the beginning, he'll have problems later on. The position of holding the flute is awkward, so you have to analyze where is the support of the flute and what supports it, so you don't put the support in the wrong place by putting it on a finger that you will need for something else. Secondly, the question of blowing. The flute is not meant to be hit with a sledge hammer. Now, no two people respond alike, but generally boys blow too hard and girls get better results.

P.E. Is the flute better suited to women then?

ZLOTNIK In a physical way—yes. A woman's jaw, chin fits and supports the flute better, but men have more prominent jaws and don't always have a place for fit there. Now, with an intermediate student, you check up to see if his foundation is good. And very often we have to go back and get some fundamentals straightened out. For instance, the question of blowing, posture, fingering, breathing and also carrying out an idea—a musical idea. If the student has an idea, he must carry it out! Even if I don't agree with him, we can discuss it. After all, you can have two or three approaches to a piece. Who is to say? However, I do insist that the player not alter the composer's directions. The composer wrote it, and that's what he felt!

P.E. But certain kinds of music, improvisation, demands the player to be an interpreter and a creator.

ZLOTNIK I think of a musician as a recreative person who is recreating the music. In baroque and in jazz you do add all sorts of ornamentations, but in the music between the nineteenth and twentieth centuries, the composer put in all kinds of directions, some of them every other bar. Composers can be mistaken. For instance, there is a concerto for flute by Ibert that has a slow movement marking which is ridiculous! If you try to play it that way, you can't manage the breathing. Now, everyone I've heard play it plays it much faster, but I tell you, my dear, that most really fine players approach the composer with respect. It's only a charlatan who will go and do all sorts of things—show himself off.

P.E. One has to surrender to the music.

ZLOTNIK Yes!

P.E. Do you have your students practice scales much?

ZLOTNIK That must be done. Nobody is born knowing the scales. Now, it is true that a good deal of music is atonal and scale practice won't help you here, but it's also true that ninety percent of the music you're going to play is diatonic music involving all kinds of scales. And you have to play them like second nature—even altered scales.

P.E. Which altered scales?

ZLOTNIK Slonimsky wrote a book in which he showed that by playing the minor scale, starting from the fifth to the fifth, you would get a different scale. It's in some way related to the modal scales. Another example is Rimsky-Korsakov, who has this arbitrary scale which alternates whole and half steps. You end up with nine tones in the scale and if you haven't played it, you go crazy because it sounds minor, but it isn't. So you learn it; otherwise, you can't play it. I find that the student's initiative to play scales becomes greater once he has acquired some facility and realized he'll acquire more by playing scales.

P.E. How does poor posture affect one's playing?

ZLOTNIK Bad posture will affect your breathing. Invariably, it cramps your diaphragm and if you sit and slouch, you won't be able to use it properly and it will affect your tone. You'll run out of air and play flat.

P.E. Do you teach your students any particular exercises for posture?

ZLOTNIK No, I just show them how to hold the flute properly. If they hold the flute right then they have good posture.

P.E. Can you tell me how you project an understanding of the various musical styles to your students?

ZLOTNIK Well, the styles can only be learned by contrast. Contrasting one style against the other. The students who remain with me long enough have to play a representative piece of the baroque, classical, romantic and contemporary periods, which includes the impressionists and others. So by the time they've learned to play four representative pieces, they also know the distinctive differences in phrasing and approach. You learn a certain staccato for Bach, but when you come to Mozart, that staccato has to be entirely different and there are differences in articulation.

P.E. Would you name some? For instance, how would baroque articulation be different from classical articulation?

ZLOTNIK Classical articulation is much crisper than Baroque articulation because the bow of the string instruments of the Baroque period was an arc bow. But by the time Mozart arrived, the modern bow had appeared and he was fascinated by it. He wrote all his pieces for this more agile bow.

P.E. What are some of the common problems a beginner has?

ZLOTNIK Usually it's learning to use the lips. Since he has to develop the muscles, and no two people develop in the same way, you have to study his particular problem and give him exercises for it. Also, if you push him too fast, he might get a charley-horse and not be able to play at all for awhile.

P.E. You have to be moderate and create a rhythm. When do you start to develop the tone?

ZLOTNIK You cannot develop tone until you have lip control. And just like you said, a rhythm has to be created. It's like weight lifting. You cannot go from a one hundred pound weight to two hundred and fifty in a few days. It takes a gradual building. So, in the beginning, you have to settle with something less than a good tone.

P.E. Would you explain this more?

ZLOTNIK For instance, I say, since in the beginning

nothing is going to sound very good, I first get the student over any phobias he may have about reaching high notes and I do this by driving him up to the top and bottom of the scale as soon as I can. Then everything is equal. This is better than having one area where he falls flat on his face and another area with a beautiful tone. Now, you can, if you want to develop a good tone, limit yourself to a small area and add one note at a time. Does it sound good? Well, it will take you thirty years. So, I say, get the student to the point where he has no phobias about going to a high or low note, then begin working on the whole thing in a small way—in little intervals.

P.E. How do you help a student rid himself of a phobia about reaching high notes?

ZLOTNIK I tell him to play deliberately to miss the note. I say, "Play as though you're going to miss it." They miss it fifty times, but pretty soon, they begin hitting it. Never get set for a note or jump for it because it won't come out.

P.E. How do you teach phrasing?

ZLOTNIK Well, what is phrasing? Phrasing is the sum total of many things. Many times people come to me and say, "I don't want to study all this baloney—I just want to study phrasing." So I ask, "How is your staccato, legato, how are your dynamics?" All of them. You've got to have the mechanics and the tools with which you are going to play. You've got to have an understanding of the composition. No amount of marking—I mean, I can mark up the phrasing but it won't help you next week when we turn the page over, because you still won't know. And if you don't know where the commas, periods, exclamation points and semi-colons belong, how are you going to build? You have to understand the structure of a piece. If the climax is here and you break your direction on the way, you've broken the tension of the whole piece. So, phrasing isn't a simple subject in itself; it's a sum total of many things.

P.E. What are the differences between phrasing in Baroque music and romantic music?

ZLOTNIK To oversimplify, you would say that in Baroque music, phrasing is a long, continuous line and in Romantic music, it's the opposite. It's like a bunch of hills and valleys, up and down, up and down. If you do it long enough, you get sea sick, but this all is a simplification of the difference.

P.E. Do you think the flute is primarily an orchestral instrument?

ZLOTNIK Yes, primarily it remains an orchestral instrument. It certainly cannot compete with the violin, piano and cello because of the limit of its repertoire.

P.E. But don't you think it's being accepted as a solo instrument again?

ZLOTNIK . . . Yes, it's changing, but for the present time, if you want to put together a concert, you'll find a limited repertoire. When you compare it to the repertoire of the violin or piano, the flute has twenty or thirty pieces at most, and of those, there are really just a few that are top notch numbers. You see, most of the big giants of the nineteenth century wrote for the piano, violin or cello.

P.E. But in the Baroque period, the flute certainly held its own and I think you will see this happen again.

ZLOTNIK Well, the Baroque period is full of flute music in part because of Frederick the Great.

P.E. Yes, he did play the flute and inspired many of the composers, but I think of Rampal's remark, that the reason we feel we have such an inadequate repertoire is that we haven't gone to the trouble of finding the pieces which are there, that we have more accepted the fact that the flute is an orchestral instrument than we actually have to.

ZLOTNIK Yes, that makes a very important point, but I think the flute hasn't come into its own yet. It's only beginning to flower now and come into its own. It has tremendous potential.

P.E. Should the flute be approached from a vocal standpoint?

ZLOTNIK Any instrument should be approached this way. People sang long before they played. That's probably why it appealed to me. It sounded like a lovely woman's voice. And it's a pure sound. That's one thing, even though we are finding many impure sounds too, I insist that my students first learn where the basic sound is; then they may make departures—whatever they want. But first know the real sound or else you'll never know it.

P.E. Do you think it's necessary to be able to imitate the masters of the flute before making your individual departure?

ZLOTNIK No. I think teaching music chronologically is wrong because it is an inhibiting method. It would be better if the fundamentals were learned by playing simple folk tunes. By learning to harmonize and what produces the harmony there. I remember the bunch of "Don't" rules that were thrown at us and the fear we had.

P.E. So you feel it's more important to understand the music—feel it than it is to imitate a master?

ZLOTNIK Oh, yes! That's what I feel. You know, contending with all that "don't" business hinders your playing, and some people studying composition can't write afterwards. Why was it that so many famous composers flunked out of their theory classes? Now, looking at this from a financial point of view, it is best that you do know how to play the accepted tone which is expected of you in an orchestra anyway. If a person goes off on a tangent and doesn't want to be affected by what other people have done before him, he'll develop his own style, but he won't be able to sell it—not in the orchestra. Conductors won't accept it because he will change the color of the music they want to play. You can't play Debussy's *Afternoon of a Faun* with a trumpet like tone. You see, if a person learns to play the accepted type sound and knows what that is, then when he wants to make departures and develops his own style, he will still be able to play anything that is required anywhere.

P.E. He'll be able to make a living.

ZLOTNIK That's right.

P.E. Do you think of the flute as a limited instrument?

ZLOTNIK If you're talking about dynamics, it certainly is when compared to the clarinet, for instance. But within its own sphere, the flute's possibilities can be developed far greater than they have been. And I think this generation will bring this about. You know, the caliber of flute playing that I hear now, as compared to when I was a youth, is much finer.

P.E. To what do you attribute this?

ZLOTNIK I think the standards of the students are much higher. And you know what is responsible for that? With a flick of a switch, a pushing of a button, anybody can hear the finest performer right in his own home and so that becomes the norm. When I was a kid, the norm was the local musicians. Maybe once or twice a year an orchestra would come to town and then, recordings were called "shellacs" and they had only one or two minutes worth of music on them. Records, then, were only lousy because they were recorded through horns—so you accepted a lower standard. Today, even in the sticks, you can have a tape recorder, stereo, cassettes ... all these things raise the standards.

P.E. Do you think students are more disciplined today?

ZLOTNIK That's hard to say, because it's such a personal thing. I know I tell my students that discipline isn't what I tell them but what they tell themselves. I've got a few anecdotes about discipline ...

P.E. Would you tell me one?

ZLOTNIK Well, we were a bunch of young fellows all attending the Damrosch Institute and I was about twenty then. Well, the day before my flute lesson one of my friends said, "Hey, we have some girls, come on, we're stepping out." "Not me, I got a lesson tomorrow." I had to practice. "Aw, come on, don't be a wet rag." "No," I said, "the good times will be there tomorrow, too. But if I goof off, who am I kidding?" Who would I be kidding? After giving up my jobs in Hartford and coming to New York to study and try to get something? They used to razz me, but some of those friends, to this day, tell me the one thing they admired most was my discipline. While I work, I work and when I play—I play. Now, it used to give me a great inner satisfaction that I had the ability to do this and not because I was told to do it.

P.E. Discipline and concentration are—

ZLOTNIK Concentration, that is one of the keys! These are the things I try to talk to my students about when I ask them what they want to do with their talent. And when they say, "I don't know." Well ... you must find a way for your talents. There was never a doubt in my mind as to what I wanted to do. The only question was, "What means do I have in order to do it?" I've been very fortunate to have been able to stick to my profession through thick and thin. And while I haven't accomplished everything, I've accomplished some of the things. So I say, "Do it, or forget it." Incidentally, talking about self-discipline, I once had a student (he was about nineteen or twenty) who played fine clarinet and saxophone. He wanted to study flute because, in the studios, you have to know how to play more than one or two instruments. Anyway, he used to hang around a bar where the musicians and contractors hung out in order to make contacts for jobs. So, one day I sat down with him and I said, "Do you think that in order to get jobs and get in with the clique, you have to sit around there and drink? That may get you a job but it's only how well you play that will make you keep it. And while you're spending time over there, you should be home practicing." You know, opportunities come along in New York, but if you're not ready, it will be a long time before the next one. So, I told him to quit bending elbows down there. Anyway, about six months later, one of the big bands came to the Paramount Theatre for an engagement. In those days there would be huge police lines and girls fainting everywhere. So, on opening day, the first alto player was taken with appendicitis. Now this was the chair where you had to play lots of clarinet, sax and flute, so they started looking around for somebody. They got the union book and they came down to this fellow, my student, and he went in. Now he'd been working hard, so he sat down and read off the book and did a terrific job. That was twenty years ago—he hasn't been out of work since. You've got to be able to deliver when they call you—not tomorrow.

P.E. What suggestions would you give to someone who wanted to teach flute?

ZLOTNIK Patience. Have patience and a great desire to do it. Of course in the beginning you'll make mistakes—like in anything else, but don't get discouraged. One thing, don't try to bluff the student. If you don't know the answer to something, just say, "Let's find out." Teaching involves quite a close relationship. There has to be mutual trust, otherwise, it won't work. A teacher has to be everything. There is really no school where you can learn to teach the flute.

P.E. What are the most common problems a teacher has to deal with in the beginning?

ZLOTNIK The flute is a perverse instrument, so this creates the problem that everything you want to do naturally, I mean, intuitively, is wrong.

P.E. Would you explain this?

ZLOTNIK You start off teaching the flute with a position that is ridiculous. Secondly, the flute gets weaker as it goes down and shriekier as it goes up. The natural tendency is to want to blow harder for the higher notes. Blowing harder has nothing to do with it. What matters are the lips.

P.E. Can the flute be self-taught?

ZLOTNIK Well, I'll tell you something—I've said this many times—if a person who is self-taught starts off with the attitude of "How can I do this with the least effort possible," he will come much closer to doing it correctly. Because, after all, the basic point in teaching is to try to get the person to do it with the least, not the most, effort.

P.E. What are the particular things to look for when buying a flute?

ZLOTNIK That's a very personal thing.

P.E. Let's say, for a beginner who needs a student flute—what should he look for?

ZLOTNIK Well, a youngster would be better off with one of the low priced American flutes that have a strong construction. Don't worry about the difference in tone quality because it won't matter much at that point. The important thing, then, is that if the flute gets a little abuse, it will stand up better. The American made flutes are the best buys. Stay away from imports. They are mostly terrible. Usually, I send my students to 48th Street where they'll pick up a flute that sells at list price for $165 or $175, but they'll pick it up for about $150 or $120.

P.E. Do you advise buying a second hand flute?

ZLOTNIK There isn't much point in buying a second hand flute because, how much cheaper can you get it and eventually it has to be fixed. So, it will cost you only twenty dollars less than a new one. But I would think anyone taking flute lessons would confer with his teacher. You see, what happens often is that they go and buy a flute without knowing much about it and they get stuck with a real lemon. Then they come to you for lessons. Now, what are you supposed to do?

P.E. What is the best way to clean the flute?

ZLOTNIK Don't touch the outside! All you'll do is hit the pads and maybe snag a spring. It's going to get tarnished, but don't worry about it. The cleaning should be done by the flute repair man. The inside you can wipe clean with the rod and a handkerchief.

P.E. How is a gold flute different in tone from a silver or platinum flute?

ZLOTNIK The importance of the material is homogeneity, whether it expands or contracts all over at the same rate, so it doesn't expand in one spot and not in another. Silver is a good conductor of heat so it will expand and contract quickly. Gold is a poor conductor and platinum even poorer. Now, the thickness of the material affects the sound. If the tube is thicker, it blows harder; if it's a thinner tube, it blows easier, so it affects the response in that respect. But no one has established what part of the material itself vibrates. Whenever the tube vibrates is when there is a sympathetic vibration, like a vase will buzz when you hit a certain tone.

P.E. Is there a difference in tone among these flutes?

ZLOTNIK That depends on the person playing. Haynes had an offer once of one thousand dollars to anybody who could recognize the difference. They put someone behind a screen and he played on wood and silver flutes—but nobody could tell the difference.

P.E. How do players of other instruments, like the saxophone, adapt to the flute?

ZLOTNIK Most of them adapt. You see, the fingering isn't a problem for them because of the first two octaves, ninety-five percent are identical. There's only a couple of fingerings that are different. Most of the players become enamoured of the flute and prefer it to their other instruments.

P.E. Why do you think this happens?

ZLOTNIK I guess it's because that by comparison, the other instruments sound raucous. You know what I mean, as far as the quality and also, it has a more homogeneous sound.

P.E. You said you started out on an old system flute; what was the changeover from this flute to the Boehm flute like?

ZLOTNIK Very difficult. Quite difficult because you not only had to change the fingerings, but the blowing was entirely different. The resistance was completely different, because it blew more easily. Therefore, you didn't need the tight embouchure as you did for the old system flute, so you had to unwind it.

P.E. How does the changing of instruments, say from saxophone to the flute, affect the embouchure?

ZLOTNIK You've got to learn to use the lips differently, so a person playing saxophone has the corners of his mouth already developed, but he's used to moving them differently. On other instruments, he has to sort of push from the upper lip down, but on the flute, you've got to push from the lower lip up. It's really a concept more than anything else. Now, the problem for the clarinet and saxophone players is the reed. With the saxophone, it isn't bad, but to play clarinet, they have to bite with the lower lip. In fact, most clarinetists have a ridge inside their lip. This ridge numbs up the lip and for flute playing, the lip has got to be very much alive. So not too many clarinetists can play good flute at the same time. Saxophone, yes, because you blow more freely on the saxophone, but the clarinet has a much more constricted embouchure.

P.E. If a person wants to learn how to play a variety of instruments, including the flute, which do you recommend he learn first?

ZLOTNIK I think you do better if you learn to play the clarinet or saxophone first. Because if you learn the flute first and then you try to learn the clarinet, you won't be able to play the flute for a year afterward. Whereas, if you learn the clarinet or saxophone first, and even though he does have the little ridge in his mouth, it won't bother him as much.

P.E. For someone who has seen many changes in music and in the flute, how do you view the new developments in flute playing and in the new music?

ZLOTNIK Well, what I've heard so far hasn't impressed me much, but it is still too new to tell and perhaps a composer will come along and write something outstanding. But one thing is that the dynamics of the flute are greatly enhanced by giving the flute a dynamic range of tremendous proportions. Since this enlarges the tone, the person playing the electric flute better have a good tone to begin with, because if it's bad, it's going to be twice as bad when electrified. The new developments are good for a fine player, but it's the poor players that use it mostly.

P.E. Has luck played an important part in your career?

ZLOTNIK Yes . . . I was lucky to get the job with Sousa before the "Crash." Lucky to be able to stay in the music business through thick and thin—but you make your own luck by doing something about it. I believe in standing on my own.

91

Talking With Flutists

JEAN-PIERRE RAMPAL
JULIUS BAKER
MARCEL MOYSE
HUBERT LAWS
DORIOT ANTHONY DWYER
HARVEY SOLLBERGER
SAMUEL BARON
PAULA ROBISON

BY PILAR ESTEVAN

VOL. I